# Know Your Heirlooms

# Know Your
# Heirlooms

### by
### Thomas H. Ormsbee

# THE McBRIDE COMPANY, Inc.
### New York

# Table of Contents

To

Clifford and Carrie
Nuttall


**You named this baby**

# Foreword

The underlying idea of this book suggested itself in the spring of 1946 when I started the syndicated newspaper feature, *Know Your Heirlooms*. This appears each week to present another facet of past American life and domesticity. Sooner or later, practically everybody falls heir to a number of articles of certain or uncertain age and value. Some give them a good home for sentimental reasons, others like them for their artistic or antique merit, and still others wonder what to do with them.

I remembered several mistakes of my youth when I passed up a few heirlooms which I would welcome heartily now. It seemed to me that a weekly column, showing a picture of a desirable heirloom and telling briefly how it reflected the life of its time and what meaning it might have for the twentieth century, would interest a scattered audience of newspaper readers.

So this newspaper feature was launched. True, there was some pessimistic comment to the effect that one might easily run out of material. That could have happened too, save for letters received from readers of the weekly installments, asking about heirlooms which they prized, with pertinent questions as to where and when the particular pieces were made, what of their value, etc.

Over the years, these letters have not only served to broaden my own outlook regarding the scope and variety of the household possessions of our forefathers, but have kept me informed as to the kinds of antiques which interest the greatest number of readers. With fair regularity, readers wrote asking when these weekly articles would appear in book form. I have now heeded that suggestion. The interests expressed in these letters brought the target into clearer focus and helped materially in choosing the selections which appear in this book. I hope at least a fair number prove to be bull's-eyes.

THOMAS H. ORMSBEE

Pound Ridge, N. Y.
November, 1956

# I

# Furniture

## *The Trestle Table in America*

THE TRESTLE TABLE is one of the furniture-making ideas which the seventeenth-century colonists brought with them from England. With a long narrow top resting on a trestle consisting of three square uprights supported by beveled block feet and made rigid by a single stretcher morticed into the uprights, it was an old and classic table form, so old indeed that Leonardo da Vinci depicted such a table in his painting, "The Last Supper."

Thus, the design of the trestle table was well-known throughout Europe even before Columbus voyaged forth in search of a shorter passage to the Indies and so found a New World. It was a design that found favor with the first colonists along the eastern seaboard of the North American continent whenever an unusually large table was required for communion use in the churches and for community functions in the houses of the period.

Quite possibly, the first Thanksgiving in the Pilgrim settlement at Plymouth was celebrated at such a table. If so, it was probably much like the one which is to be seen in the American Wing of the Metropolitan Museum of Art in New York (Illustration 1). This table is generally conceded to be the oldest one of American make still in existence. Its top is a single white pine plank and its understructure is all of native white oak. Unusually large, twelve feet long by two feet wide and twenty-nine inches tall, it was probably made for church use about 1650 or even earlier.

Other trestle tables of smaller size were made in most of the New England colonies throughout the rest of the seventeenth and well into the eighteenth centuries, especially in farming communities. All have the same primitive austerity of design and a one-piece top. Few have survived, but some may remain unrecognized and unappreciated in shed or storage room waiting to be found

9

by a person familiar with their distinctive trestle structure and knot-free board top.

The trestle table went out of fashion about 1730. Sixty years later, the Shakers revived it for use in their religious communal dwellings, beginning about 1790 and continuing for some thirty years. It is these Shaker-made examples that one is most likely to acquire today. Even they are rarities, though not as rare as the earlier ones. It is not hard to identify them. First, the top consists of two to four boards, with or without transverse cleats at the ends, instead of the one-piece pine plank. The understructure also differs. The trestles are lighter and the connecting stretcher is placed immediately beneath the top, instead of halfway between top and floor. The woods used are also different. Oak is never used. Trestles and stretcher are of a straight-grain maple or sometimes yellow birch. The boards that form the top are either maple or white pine. Sizes of these Shaker tables vary from twenty feet to about eight feet long, the smaller ones being just over four feet in length.

From the viewpoint of the collector, any trestle table is worth having, whether of Shaker origin or earlier.

### The Eighteenth-Century Gate-Leg Table

The gate-leg was the first sophisticated table design of American cabinetmakers. It was also the first with drop leaves. This change in design came about 1690 when these craftsmen began to produce drop-leaf tables with an understructure of baluster-turned members. It was a table form that had been used in England for some fifty years before it came into favor in the American colonies.

Its descriptive name comes from the gate-like form of the two swing legs which support the raised leaves. This type of table ranges in size from the small occasional ones which, when closed, occupy so little space as to earn the name "tuckaways," to very large ones which can seat twelve to fourteen people. The small tables usually have a circular top; that of the larger sizes is either oval or oblong. The center fixed leaf is rectangular and relatively narrow. It is attached to the understructure of turned legs and stretcher members and has a single drawer within the bed. The two movable or drop leaves are attached to the long sides of the fixed one by hinges, their matching edges being finished with a concave-convex beading known as a knuckle joint.

The understructure, of which the swinging gates are a part, consists of four stationary and two swinging legs that are baluster-turned in vase-and-ring (Illustration 2) or kindred turnings and terminate in ball, pear-shape, knob or, less often, carved Spanish feet. Just above these feet the legs are braced by a box stretcher with members of the same type of turning as the legs. The two swinging legs have similar braces, and their upper ends are mortice-and-tenon joined to horizontals on which the leaves rest when raised. The inner ends of braces and stretchers are pivot-joined to the main framework so that they swing out to a maximum of 90 degrees to support the raised leaves.

Gate-leg tables were made by American cabinetmakers from as early as 1690 to about 1730 with simpler ones of the survival sort for possibly twenty years longer. They were produced in all sections of the American colonies from

Pennsylvania northward. Walnut was usual for those made south of New England. Plain or curly maple or a combination of maple and cherry were favored by New England craftsmen.

With a few very large tables, the drop leaves are each supported by a pair of swinging gates, but these are much rarer than examples with single gates. Usually the gate-leg was used as the family dining table, placed in the center of the large main room which did duty as both living and dining room. Because of constant use, the upper surfaces of stretcher members are usually worn down, sometimes nearly flat, from the generations of feet that have rested on them during mealtime—a sign of age and normal wear. Feet, of ball or other shape, are also apt to be partially worn away.

### The Rare Butterfly Table

The butterfly table, as it has been called for the last fifty or seventy-five years, takes its name from the two wing-like swinging brackets that support the leaves of the top (Illustration 3). Whether the craftsman who originated it had a butterfly in mind when he designed these brackets is a question. Although simple in construction and restrained in ornamental details of leg turnings, shaping of top, and leaf supports, such tables have definite appeal. When one of them is offered for sale, its price can approach that of an ornate and richly carved pie-crust table of the American Chippendale period.

There are reasons for the scarcity of the butterfly table. It dates from about 1700 to 1730 in the early years of American cabinetmaking. It was made only in southern New England—Connecticut, parts of Massachusetts, and possibly Rhode Island. Original demand for it seems not to have extended beyond the area of its making. It was probably an occasional table designed for use in the best room of a simple home.

Surviving examples are small, being from two to four inches lower than gate-leg tables of the same period and with a top about thirty-six inches long and from forty to forty-four inches wide when the leaves are raised. Butterfly table tops are usually oval, oblong, or square; rarely are they round. Woods used were maple or cherry for the top and various native hard woods for legs, stretchers, and other parts of the base. In their original state, they were painted and so a variety of woods did not matter.

Structurally, this little table is related to the simple joined stool of the middle and late seventeenth century. Both have simple vase-turned legs with an outward slant, a plain box stretcher connecting the legs close to the floor and below this simple knob feet. Obviously the unknown craftsman took the joined stool as model and, in slightly larger form, put a table top on it with drop leaves and supporting brackets of curving, wing-like shape. The latter were socketed into the side of the stretcher and the upper cross members of the bed so that they swung out and in readily. The inner edge of each of these brackets was straight and was given the same slant as the legs.

Nearly always, in the bed was a narrow oblong drawer, the bottom wider than the top, which slid in from one end. It was equipped with a simple wooden knob similar to the feet in turning. Made over two hundred years ago in a small area and for a limited clientele, it is proof that our early cabinetmakers had originality and a good eye for restrained beauty. It was no memory piece either, since England made no table like it. Though rare, it is deservedly popular with anyone lucky enough to own or find an example.

These originals should not be confused with the coffee or occasional table adaptations produced by present-day furniture factories from about 1920. They are smaller, generally of mahogany and of much lighter construction.

### The Pembroke Table, American Version

In the early 1750's Thomas Chippendale of London, England, designed a table with broad bed and shallow leaves, Its four straight legs were connected by an X-shaped stretcher. Intended as a tea table, he gave it the name "Pembroke" in honor of the client for whom he designed it.

It appeared in his book, *The Gentleman and Cabinet Maker's Director,* and very soon American cabinetmakers had taken this highly stylized design, given it their usual editing and produced a version that remained in favor with their public for a full seventy years. Cabinetmakers in the urban centers made very handsome ones with leaves either plain or serpentine in outline. Square chamfered legs were braced by either flat or arched X-stretchers that sometimes were delicately carved in Chinese fretwork patterns (Illustration 4). Fretwork brackets often decorated the joining of legs and skirt. There was also a wide shallow drawer framed with narrow cockle-bead molding at one end of the table bed. Mahogany was of course the favored wood, though some tables, especially the early ones, were walnut.

Country-made Pembrokes followed the same general lines of construction but left off such furbelows as fretwork carving of stretchers or openwork brackets. The table in Illustration 5 is a better-than-average country piece. It was made in Maine about 1790 or some years after this ornate style passed out of favor in such centers as Philadelphia, New York, and Boston. In rural areas where the older style still lingered, enough of the new had pentrated for cabinetmakers to add a few transitional touches, such as a slight taper to the hitherto square leg of Chippendale or a brass rosette drawer-pull instead of the earlier bail handle.

In a very few years the Hepplewhite version of this table appeared with characteristic tapered leg and sometimes without the diagonal stretchers of the Chippendale years. Mahogany was still the favored wood and city-made pieces were decorated with satinwood inlay. Country Pembrokes were plainer, sometimes of cherry or other hard woods. About the turn of the century came the Sheraton style with its slender turned and reeded legs ending in brass castered feet.

This deservedly popular table went out of style about 1815 when the American Empire fashion took over, but again country craftsmen did not relinquish it so readily. For a good fifteen years longer they made a fair number of very simple Pembrokes of such native hard woods as cherry, plain or fancy grained maple, walnut, or yellow birch. This survival type had the broad bed and narrow leaves of the table designed by Chippendale sixty or seventy years before. But the leaves were straight with square or rounded corners and there was usually no drawer in the table bed. Legs were either the slender tapering ones of the Hepplewhite influence or the turned but unreeded legs of the Sheraton style. It was severely plain but still a Pembroke. Today this very quality, added to general usefulness, make it a welcome addition to the modern home.

Although Chippendale's book of furniture designs was owned and used by many of the leading American cabinetmakers, few of them did much with those in the Chinese manner. The characteristic fretwork, an interlaced pattern done either in pierced silhouette or carved in low relief, was an intricate detail to be attempted only by an experienced and able craftsman. It was expensive and, moreover, a slavish copy of Chinese Chippendale designs would have been too ornate for American tastes.

One of the few who adapted this detail in a manner palatable to American taste was John Townsend of Newport, Rhode Island. He took Chippendale's Pembroke design with its wide bed and shallow leaves, gave it a plain rectangular outline, set it on square legs ornamented with fluting and connected them with a saltire stretcher ornamented in a simple geometric fretwork pattern. He also added fretwork brackets at the joinings of legs and bed. Every detail, intricate or plain, reflected the original Chippendale design with an American accent.

He made this table (Illustration 4) between 1760 and 1770. Born in 1732, he saw the end of the Chippendale era but was still young enough to adjust to the new styles of Hepplewhite and Sheraton and his skill and artistic ability produced furniture as light and delicate as the earlier style was sturdy and elaborate.

### The Protecting Settle

Take a bench, add a high back and side pieces and you have a settle. A simple piece which could be made by anyone handy with tools, by late Tudor years it had become common in English manors and farmhouses. It was placed near the great open fireplace at right angles to the hearth. There, protected from drafts by the tall back and solid ends, its occupants could toast in comfort.

By the time the first colonists left for America, the settle was an accepted and necessary piece of country furniture. So, as our early pioneers erected the first modest houses and made the essential furniture items, the settle was one of the important pieces. The oak of old England was lacking but there was plenty of native wood.

Pine or other soft wood was the favored material since it was easy to work and, as the settle was a strictly utilitarian piece, no time was wasted on carving. It did not matter if more than one kind of wood was used, since the finish was a coat of paint, frequently greenish blue. Sometimes there was storage space underneath the seat (Illustration 6). Sometimes there was a shelf at the back for accommodating a candle. But the average examples were just settles and nothing more.

Surviving English settles date from no earlier than the end of the reign of Elizabeth I. These have a low paneled back, sometimes handsomely carved, and arms at either end that resemble those of chairs of the time, showing that settles, settees and sofas are merely elongated chairs.

In America, with the more rigorous climate and drafty houses, there was

13

no shortening of the hooded back, and the side pieces bore little resemblance to either wainscot or slat-back chair arms. Settles here were pioneer furniture. They were part of country home furnishings from 1650 on through the eighteenth century along the Atlantic seaboard and appeared in homes along the westward trek during the early 1800's as well. Being of soft wood and in constant use, the majority were worn out or destroyed.

As a result, old settles are scarce items today. They are worth owning, especially for use in old country homes. That any made during the seventeenth century are still around is most unlikely but those of the eighteenth and early nineteenth centuries are desirable, especially since these pieces were unaffected by changing styles. Variations in treatment of side pieces, paneling of back or other details were the ideas of individual makers. In such manner does a humble piece have much in common with its more pretentious relatives, the sofa and the settee.

### The Puritan Century Wainscot Chair

It is generally conceded that the little group of Pilgrims who set foot on Plymouth Rock over 335 years ago brought practically no household furnishings with them. But the memory of the simple pieces of furniture they had known in their English provincial homes was still vivid.

Consequently, as soon as they had proper houses, their cabinetmakers, then known as "joiners," began making the provincial furniture to which they were accustomed, such as the wainscot chair, the turned spindle chair, and the slat-back. Of these, the wainscot chair is the most formal. No house had more than one and that would only be found in the home of an important and prosperous man.

Chairs were few and far between during the first forty years of colonization. Those few were of the armchair type, reserved for Father as head of the house. Such lesser folk as women and children sat on stools and so made their backs strong and straight. For that matter, Father was more grand than comfortable, since his chair, whether architectural or turned in construction, had a straight uncompromising back and a plain, flat board seat, painfully hard to moderns accustomed to springs and cushions. Chairs were not designed for comfort but as a mark of distinction.

English chairs were no more comfortable at that time. Some of them were handsomely carved but the same type of construction held: a stout underbody with front posts turned, substantial box stretchers at top and bottom, plain board seat, arms curving downward slightly from the back and the back itself either covered completely with an elaborate carved design or plain with a carved panel in geometric pattern.

The name wainscot reflects its construction, particularly the back which, like woodwork used for room walls, is constructed of panelwork framed by stiles and rails. Apparently only a limited number of wainscots were made in America. Those few were produced in New England of native white oak. A very few were also brought over from England about 1630 to 1640 during the height of the Puritan migration and in a measure served as models for some of the more elaborate pieces made here.

14

The chair in Illustration 7 is an example of an English provincial wainscot found in manor houses at the time. Of oak with simple detail and sturdy construction, it was made about 1650. The simple carving of back panel and cresting mark its rural origin. The small knob or ball feet have disappeared through three centuries of use, making the box-shape stretcher very close to the floor. Except for its restored seat, it is all original. Several coats of oil followed by waxing have given it a fine soft finish.

Plain or elaborate, most antique wainscots are apt to be in museum collections or owned by schools and colleges for use on ceremonial occasions. Sometimes one may be seen in a private home as a living-room or library chair where it is not really as uncomfortable as it looks and can at least serve as a conversation piece.

### How Turned Chairs Were Made

The turned chairs produced by American craftsmen for fully two centuries are of three kinds, the slat-back, the spindle-back, and the corner or roundabout (Illustration 8). This got its name from the fact that the seat was set on the diagonal thus making a chair that fitted easily into the corner of a room.

As we seldom see one of these chairs stripped of its seat of either twisted rush or woven splint, we do not often have the chance of examining the structure. If the stripped corner chair illustrated is studied for a minute or two, it becomes evident that all its parts, except for the surmounting U-shaped arm, are simple turned or square members, each with its function.

This chair structure has much in common with the steel skeleton of a modern building before it has been encased in concrete and masonry. But where steel work is held together by rivets, the uprights, seat rails, and stretchers of this chair are joined by either mortice and tenon or socket joints made tight by wooden pegs driven into bored holes. The result is a chair of simple construction and great strength with ornamentation achieved by vase-shaped and ring turnings of uprights and stretchers. Originally this chair had small knob or pear-shaped feet which have disappeared, either worn away through use or cut off to lower the height of the seat from seventeen to about fifteen inches.

Structurally, the other two types of chairs were made of much the same turned parts and put together with pegged mortice and tenon or socket joints. With the slat-back, as the name implies, the back was formed of three to five slightly concave horizontal slats. The spindle-back had slender simply-turned spindles placed vertically and socketed into the top and bottom cross-pieces.

These turned chairs were made very early in America—by 1650 or before, and continued to be produced by country craftsmen until 1860. Among the last were the slat-back rocking chairs which the Shakers first made for their own use and later peddled in considerable quantity from town to town in New England and New York State.

Making corner or roundabout chairs started about 1720 and continued for about a hundred years. Many were made for taverns as they were well-suited for the hard use they underwent in the tap room. Maple was the chief wood used but some were made of an assortment of native hardwoods, such as ash, oak, birch, and beech. Such chairs were frequently painted a bottle green or finished with New England red filler. Since this was the intended finish, what or how many different woods were used did not matter. Consequently, the old craftsmen took what woods were at hand in turning out parts, providing they were well-seasoned and free from knots or other blemishes that might reduce the necessary strength.

### The Writing-Arm Windsor

"One of commodious seat having a bracket with a drawer underneath in which one can keep quills and sand, the bracket is useful to hold our account books and other papers and enables us to quote from the books those things that need our attention," wrote a Philadelphian in 1763. He was describing a writing-arm Windsor which he had admired at the home of a friend, and which he promptly ordered for himself from "Richmond on Sassafras Street, a joiner of much repute who has come out from the motherland."

Windsor chairs had first appeared in Philadelphia nearly forty years before and had soon become so popular that craftsmen specializing in their making were found in growing numbers elsewhere, especially in New England and New York. This variation of the Windsor appears also to have originated in Philadelphia and to have remained in favor for almost a hundred years.

A novelty in the 1760's, the first of them probably had a detachable writing arm. Then came the sturdier, broad writing tablet, rigid or swinging, which was an integral part of the chair. Further developments included small drawers attached to the underside of either the writing tablet or seat and quite often a candlestick slide, usually at the outer end of the writing arm.

This ingenious piece is an excellent example of the way American craftsmen adapted furniture to serve special needs. The Windsor chair as originally made in England was itself an adaptation since it was largely the work of wheel-wrights. Using the tools and technique for fashioning a wagon wheel, they transformed the spokes into spindles, the rim, steamed and bent, into the curved arm and the hub into a thick, one-piece seat, often saddled to be body-conforming. Legs, spindles, and arm were put together with socket joints as with the parts of a wheel.

From the number of books recording life in America during colonial times, from the quantities of personal correspondence and the scores of account ledgers that have survived, it is apparent that, from an early date, Americans were much addicted to taking pen in hand. This characteristic became especially pronounced in the years between 1760 and 1775. Men in New England wanted to know what was happening in the other colonies, just as those living in the latter were keen to learn what their New England contemporaries were thinking and doing. Letter mail of that time was considerably swelled as a result. Not all of it was penned at desks or secretaries.

The writing-arm Windsor by no means took the place of a desk but it was a convenient adjunct, one that could be moved about easily to a spot where the light was better or pulled close to the fire on a cold day. Made to suit the taste of the individual buyer, design details varied. One originally owned by Thomas Jefferson is a simple comb-back with a plain writing tablet having neither drawer nor candle slide. Its distinctive feature is a revolving

(*Illustration 1*) Seventeenth-century American Trestle Table. Single board pine top is about twelve feet long and two feet wide. Understructure is of oak.

*(Illustration 2)* Above, Large New England Gate-Leg Table, ca. 1720.

*(Illustration 3)* Below, A Connecticut Butterfly Table, ca. 1710-1725.

*(Illustration 4)* **An American Chippendale Pembroke Table. Of mahogany, it was made by John Townsend, Newport, R. I., ca. 1760-1770.**

*(Illustration 5)* **Transition Chippendale-Hepplewhite Pembroke Table. Made in Maine, ca. 1790. The taper of legs indicate the shift to the latter style period.**

*(Illustration 6)* **A Hooded Pine Settle from New England, ca. 1750. Made of plain boards. The curved outline of the ends and the three drawers beneath the seat are unusual refinements.**

*(Illustration 7)* A Provincial English Wainscot Chair, ca. 1650.

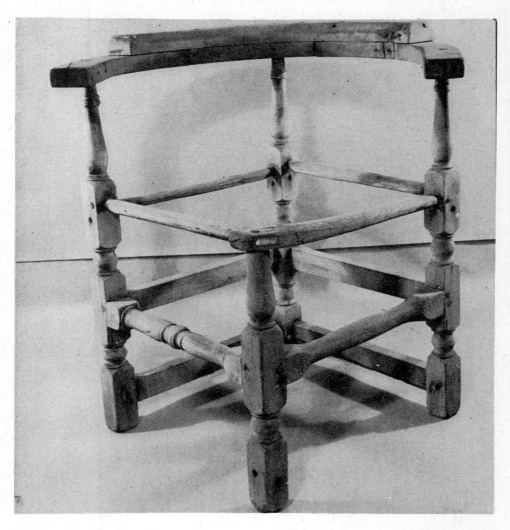

*(Illustration 8)* Frame of Turned Corner Chair. Stripped of its rush seat. The sturdy pegged joints show clearly.

*(Illustration 9)* **A Comb-Back Writing-Arm Windsor. A Connecticut example, ca. 1760-1775.**

*(Illustration 10)* **A Rod-Back Writing Windsor, New England, ca. 1800. Beneath the broad arm is shallow drawer for stationery. At its outer end is a candle slide.**

*(Illustration 11)* **Arrow-Back Windsor with Original Rockers.**

*(Illustration 12a)* **An Unusual Hitchcock Chair Grained to Resemble Maple.**

*(Illustration 12b)* **Hitchcock Chair Painted to Resemble Rosewood.**

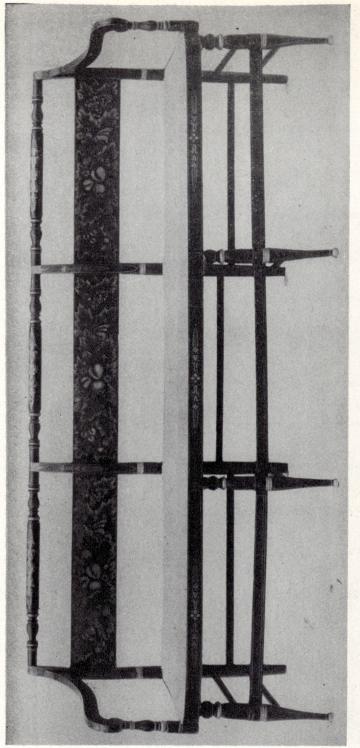

(*Illustration 13*) An Eight-Leg Hitchcock Settee. Its ornamentation in stencil gilding is more elaborate than usual, particularly the fruit and leafage on the three-piece splat of the back.

(*Illustration 14*) A Cape Cod Rocker by Hitchcock. A baby could be rocked to sleep safely if placed behind the removable fence at the left. A few were made for twins with fences at each end.

*(Illustration 15)* An American Bible Box. This is a survival example, and is of pine with hand-wrought nails, made ca. 1800. Note the lock set in the lid which is unusual.

*(Illustration 16)* Pennsylvania Dutch Bridal Chest. Between the two elaborate panels is the inscription "Jacob Rickert, Anno 1782."

seat similar to the modern office armchair. It must be dated before 1776 since in it was written the first draft of the Declaration of Independence.

Benjamin Franklin, who had his finger in so many inventive pies, was apparently satisfied with the plainest of writing-arm Windsors without carving on comb or elaborate spindle turnings. The writing arm was rigid and supported by three turned uprights.

These specially made chairs were produced in the comb-back first and then in the low-back, bow-back, and rod-back types. Never made in such quantity as the regular armchair Windsors a good number of comfortably-off households had them. Turnings of legs, stretchers and spindles and other details reflected those common to Pennsylvania, New York and New England provenance. From these details, date and place of making can often be determined. For instance, the comb-back and low-back types were mostly made in Philadelphia and could be dated between 1760 and 1790.

New England was partial to the bow-back from 1760 to 1820, although other types were made there such as the comb-back (Illustration 9). This chair was made between 1760 and 1775 in Connecticut as indicated by the leg-turnings with longer halves tapering sharply from the baluster-shaping above. The same turnings are repeated in the front-arm upright and those supporting the writing tablet. The chair still retains its original bottle green paint, the color most often used for finishing Windsors in New England.

The rod-back, showing the influence of the Sheraton period, was in favor from about 1800 to 1830 (Illustration 10). After that, the heavy continuous-arm Windsor with horse-shoe back, appeared. This less desirable type was a revival of the earlier low-back type and was also made with the writing arm until about 1860.

### Developments of the Windsor Chair

At the hands of American cabinetmakers the Windsor chair developed six different types during its first seventy-five years here without benefit of prevailing styles. This chair with solid plank seat, spindle back, and canted legs was so sturdy and yet so well-adapted to the human body that the reasons for its popularity from 1725, when it first appeared in Philadelphia, on down to the present day are not hard to find. Yet in its country of origin, provincial England, it never advanced beyond the status of farmhouse or tavern furniture.

In America, the making of Windsor chairs soon became a specialized craft with a considerable number of cabinetmakers producing no other furniture and styling themselves "Windsor chairmakers." It was already a perfectly designed style. They had only to add nice details, such as turnings, finer shaping of the saddle seat, graceful carving on arms and combpieces, and various individual touches which made the work of each maker distinctive.

The early low-back type of Windsor, with its horseshoe-shaped continuous arm into which short rod spindles were fitted, gave no support above the small of one's back, so chairs supporting more of the body were soon developed. These were the comb-back, bow-back, fan-back and arch-back. Originally a thoroughly masculine chair, the fan-back was the first type to be made in a

**17**

smaller or "lady" chair. This happened about 1750 when the Windsor of humble origin had become handsome enough to appear anywhere except in the drawing room of a mansion.

By the start of the nineteenth century, there was little left to do for the Windsor except to add a few touches of the current Sheraton furniture style. These presently showed up in two types, known as the rod-back and the arrow-back. Here the straight lines of Sheraton were to be seen in the bamboo-turned box stretcher, the squarish seat, and sloping back with rod spindles. The rod-back was made in arm and side chair forms and occasionally as a rocking chair.

The arrow-back was likewise made in these forms. It was also the only Windsor made in quantity as a rocking chair. Windsors of the six earlier types are sometimes found with rockers but they are usually a later addition with rockers very close to the H stretcher, showing that from two to four inches, had been cut off the legs to allow for this change. The arrow-back, a variation of the slightly earlier rod-back, takes its name from the three to five narrow, arrow-shaped vertical splats that are part of the back and fit into the flat crest rail.

In the chair shown in Illustration 11, the back is surmounted by a slightly arched combpiece that is stencil-decorated in colors and gilt with a striped shield flanked by foliage scrolls. Five slender spindles, slightly concave and vertically striped, support it and are attached to the upper side of the wide top rail. There are four flattened arrow-shaped spindles socketed into back rail and seat. The short rockers show the signs of more than a century of use, their centers being worn nearly flat by the rhythmic rocking to and fro of five generations. Arrow-backs were made from about 1810 to 1835, with and without arms, with and without combpiece and with or without rockers.

### Lambert Hitchcock, Chairmaker

About a hundred and thirty years ago, a young Connecticut Yankee with an eye to business left his native town of Cheshire and settled in the northern part of the Nutmeg State where he established a chair factory near a branch of the Farmington River. His name was Lambert Hitchcock. He was descended from a Hitchcock who had been part of the Puritan exodus from England, and his family had lived in and near New Haven since 1639.

His factory began in a modest way by making chair parts which were shipped chiefly to Charleston, South Carolina, and other southern cities. The business grew rapidly and it was not long before there was enough of a settlement around the industry to warrant giving it the name of Hitchcockville. By 1822 he had stopped shipping chair parts and had begun making chairs, particularly the painted "fancy" sort which is now synonymous with his name.

The design of this chair originated with Thomas Sheraton and such chairs were made in America when Hitchcock was still a boy. American chairmakers modified the design to suit their public and these simple chairs became popular in New England, New York, and as far west as Ohio. Hitchcock originated no design but, like his fellow craftsmen, modified those in vogue. For instance, the seats of his chairs are wider in front than in back. The rung between the two front legs was delicately turned and the backs had a curved top (Illustration 12). Treatment of the broad back splat also varied. It was a simple chair, well made and easy to handle. That and the hand-done stencil decoration of the back was probably what kept them in favor for the thirty-odd years of their making, and today finds them cherished, especially in sets of six or eight, in the modern home.

At the height of his career, Hitchcock had a hundred or more employees—men, women, and children. The men made the chairs, the women did the stencil decoration, and the children put on the first coat of paint, always a dark red .Hitchcock made a good chair and took enough pride in his work to put his name on the wooden strip at the back of the rush seat. Today the name "Hitchcock" is applied to this type of painted chair, whether it bears his label or not.

Naturally, however, a chair marked "L. Hitchcock, Warranted," "L. Hitchcock, Hitchcockville, Ct.," or "Hitchcock, Alford & Co., is more valuable than an unlabeled one. Also it fixes the approximate date when it was made. A chair bearing the third label would date between 1829 and 1843, the years when Lambert was in partnership with his brother-in-law, Alfred Alford.

In addition to the popular side chair, Hitchcock made an eight-legged settee with a triple connected back that showed its close relation to the painted "fancy" chair (Illustration 13). Also made at his factory were Boston rockers, settees equipped with rockers, and the Cape Cod rocker or settee cradle. Indeed he was one of the first to make rocking chairs as a factory product. Before the 1820's rockers were made separately and added to a straight chair, which was probably what happened when Benjamin Franklin realized that these appendages need not be confined exclusively to cradles.

The Cape Cod rocker was a contemporary of the Boston rocker, being made from about 1825 to 1850. It was a settee on rockers with stencil decoration similar to the Boston rocker and the painted "fancy" chair. Added to it was a fence-like attachment which transformed one end of it into a cradle. (Illustration 14). It was one of the few labor-saving devices of the early nineteenth century. The baby could be laid on a pillow and the mother could sit at the other end, catch up on her sewing, knitting or other stint, and rock a child and herself in comfort.

Such pieces were produced mostly in New England, Hitchcockville being one of the factories making them but by no means the only one. A rarity among them is one designed for twins. With this, the fence attachments were two in number and placed at either end. The baby sitter occupied the space in the middle. She may or may not have had much time for either knitting or sewing.

### The Bible Box, Ancestor of the Desk

Among the wooden chests which made up the luggage of the first American colonists were small dual-purpose boxes of oak. Equipped with a large lock, such a box would be ornamented on the front with shallow carving and also have the initials of its owner carved just below the lock. Stored within were a bulky quarto-size Bible, seeds for planting in the new land, family trinkets, and writing materials, since it was the early substitute for a desk.

19

When it was placed on a joined stool or small table, its lid could serve as a writing tablet. This arrangement held until close to the end of the century when the desk first appeared as a separate piece of furniture although still resembling its parent. It was in two parts and consisted of a larger and more detailed writing box, with slanting lid, placed on a frame. From this beginning the desk evolved, taking various forms from the one-piece bureau to the secretary.

Meanwhile, the Bible or writing box did not pass wholly from the scene. Not everyone could afford a desk. Furthermore, these boxes, which had been brought over from England and Holland, were well-made and of a convenient size for storing small prized possessions. So, from about 1650 to 1800, New England cabinetmakers, working mostly in Massachusetts and Connecticut, continued to make them, using oak and pine as material and following the proportions, construction, and decorative details of the imported boxes.

Few of these seventeenth-century writing boxes are now found outside museum collections. Survival examples dating from the eighteenth century and probably made by country cabinetmakers turn up occasionally. Those made up to 1725 are apt to be of walnut and are uncarved; later, pine was a favored wood. The box in Illustration 15 is entirely of pine and probably the work of a farmer handy with tools. It is a little shallower than the early boxes but the proportions are similar. The base is flat instead of molded and hand wrought iron nails take the place of dovetail joints. Pin-and-batten strip hinges fasten the lid. This is most unusual. There is no decoration except for shallow scratch work, probably done with a scribing awl, of two circles on the front enclosing the initials J.A.

In this box, dating from before 1815, the unknown maker probably kept his account books, his writing paper, and any articles important enough to be under lock and key.

### Pennsylvania Dutch, Plain and Fancy

Furniture made by the Pennsylvania Dutch and used in the ample houses of their prosperous farms displays two of the dominant characteristics of these folk. Their fondness for colorful ornamentation in the home is evident in fine examples of painted furniture, such as the bridal chest, shown in Illustration 16. Their hard-headed practicality, on the other hand, is demonstrated by the simple lines and sturdy construction of such pieces made for everyday use as the water bench (Illustration 17).

Originally the water bench was a purely functional piece of kitchen furniture, reflecting the farm life of the Pennsylvania Dutch before the days of plumbing and piped-in water. Such benches were indigenous to the five counties back of Philadelphia which were settled mainly by that close-knit group of late seventeenth and early eighteenth-century emigrants from the Rhine Valley, originally listed as Dutch because they had embarked at Rotterdam.

Most water benches date from between 1800 and 1860 and still retain the Continental flavor of the German Palatinate. Their original use is indicated by their name. Existing as they did in the era of the old oaken bucket, the counter shelf held the wash basin and pails of fresh water brought from the well or spring. Other buckets and pails were kept in the cupboard below. Dippers and basins were put on the narrow top shelf which was fitted into scroll-cut ends eighteen to twenty inches above. Three drawers immediately below held soap and other small toilet articles.

A typical example was made of pine, sometimes combined with other soft woods. The general outline is similar to a Welsh dresser but neither as tall nor as completely shelved. Most pieces have only the top and counter shelves. (The middle shelf in the bench illustrated is unusual and may be a later addition). Total height of the piece varies from forty-six to forty-eight inches.

General use of the water bench as part of Pennsylvania Dutch kitchen equipment ceased about 1900, but these thrifty people were not foolish enough to reduce such good sturdy pieces to kindling. Consequently there were enough of them in existence to satisfy demand when someone realized about twenty years ago that a well-proportioned water bench could be moved into the dining room and serve either as a dresser for displaying a collection of pewter or as a buffet.

Water benches have now become especially popular in informal country homes because of their good lines and adaptability, and antique dealers from all sections of the country have gone to the Pennsylvania Dutch area to acquire examples. As a result, such pieces can be found from New England to the Pacific Coast. Although they were originally painted Amish blue or some other typical color, the general practice today is to refinish them in the natural pine as better suited to the advanced social station of this once lowly piece.

Bridal chests date from about 1760-1830. They were made of pine or poplar by local carpenters and decorated by self-taught artists. As such they were folk art and represented a love of color and a partiality to symbolism inherent in these people. Structurally, the chests are rectangular boxes with hinged lids, usually supported on four plain bracket feet. The main decorative effect was attained by painted designs on the front consisting of two or three panels. Here symbolism played an important part as did love of nature. Certain motifs are distinctive of each of the five counties in which these German refugees from the Rhine Valley settled.

For instance, the chest in Illustration 16 has two arched panels enclosing parrot-like birds with tulips and fuchsias, a design common to Lancaster County. The ground color is a reddish brown. Other favored ground colors are Amish blue and cypress green. Designs common to the other counties are: arched panels flanked by a pair of unicorns rampant among tulips and pomegranates, from Berks County; square panels filled with flower sprays rising from a vase, from Dauphin County; large circular medallions overlaid with six-pointed stars, often flanking an arched central panel lettered with owner's name, from Lehigh County; and square panels with tulips and carnations, from Montgomery County.

Many of the designs were painted by men who made a specialty of such decoration and traveled from town to town. Dauphin County had two, Christian Selzer and Johann Rank. In Lancaster County there was Heinrich Otto, also well-known for his *fractur* writing. A chest decorated and signed by him or either of the other two men would obviously be most desirable and valuable.

Pursuit of the fox with horse and hound was indirectly responsible for a long-legged piece of furniture known as a hunt board. Fox hunting as a sport became popular in England about the middle of the eighteenth century; in America there was the usual lag in time, further increased by the unsettled conditions during the Revolutionary War. By the late 1780's the former colonies south of Pennsylvania were beginning to take an interest in the sport.

Country gentlemen of Maryland, Virginia, the Carolinas, and Georgia took pride in the quality of their hunters and packs of hounds. The area was ideally suited to fox hunting and the sport was taken seriously until well into the third quarter of the nineteenth century. As these fox hunts began at dawn and sometimes lasted until sunset, the horsemen naturally returned tired, hungry, and saddlesore to the house where food and drink waited.

These were informal occasions when the mud-spattered horsemen who came direct from the chase stood around and ate, buffet-style, while they talked over the day's sport. A tall sideboard on which the weary huntsman could lean an elbow while he ate was the ideal piece of furniture and so the hunt board evolved. It was placed either in the back hall or in one of the detached buildings that served as the plantation office.

Hunt boards were made of native woods such as pine, walnut, butternut, cherry, or maple, either alone or combined. The first crude ones may have been made by slaves on the various plantations. As the idea gained popularity, local cabinetmakers produced them and added their own individual touches that made them good, bad or indifferent, according to the skill, or lack of it, of the maker. In essence, the piece is a tall sideboard, forty to forty-eight inches high, with a central cupboard surrounded by drawers (Illustration 18). Arrangement of the drawers varies. Most hunt boards have deep ones on either side of the central "cabin." Sometimes there are two or more shallow drawers above, sometimes none. Occasionally a cabinetmaker of more than average skill produced a piece that followed so closely the design and arrangement of the conventional sideboard that only its height marks it as designed for the back hall instead of the dining room.

Hunt boards still extant date from about 1800 to 1850. Their designs, always along simple lines, are in the manner of Hepplewhite and Sheraton.

Among the heirlooms reflecting a definite social and economic custom of the past is the sugar chest. A southern piece, made during the eighteenth and early nineteenth centuries, it was primarily a chest on legs, fitted with a bin for sugar, another for coffee, and quite often small drawers for spices.

Since these were all luxuries, the chest was therefore fitted with a lock. In the agricultural South, especially Kentucky and Tennessee, each plantation was self-sufficient as far as food products went, except for sugar, tea, coffee, and spices. Quite aside from the money value of these items, which was considerable, poor transportation made delivery possible only once or twice a year. Therefore, stern rationing was necessary on a plantation with numerous dependents. Sorghum, honey, and molasses were sweetening substitutes for everyday use.

Except for a limited amount of cane sugar grown in Louisiana, all brown and white sugar used in colonial America and later in the United States was imported and remained costly until nearly 1870. The less refined brown type was doled out by the housewife each day for cooking and ordinary use; white sugar which came in a cone, wrapped in a deep violet-colored paper, was for company. Cutting it into pieces for serving was not entrusted to servants, as precious grains of it might be wasted. There were special cutters or shears for the process which were wielded by the mistress of the house or her daughters.

Most of the sugar chests were plantation-made and vary considerably in quality and workmanship. Some are merely crude boxes on legs; others are expertly fashioned and even decorated with inlay. Other furniture forms besides the plain chest were used. Quite a few are found in the form of a desk or even a secretary; still others resemble primitive highboys. All had the bin arrangement and, with few exceptions, were well-equipped with locks to guard the luxury items stored within.

Native woods were used, with walnut and cherry especially favored. Nicely finished and decorated sugar chests were probably kept in the dining room, quite near the sideboard, and may have doubled as mixing stands for the juleps and toddies that were part of southern hospitality. The sugar chest in Illustration 19 is typical of most of these pieces which, like the hunt board, are a southern invention. Here the chest has the general outline of the late seventeenth-century blanket chest which continued to be made for close to two hundred years. The well where blankets would normally be stored is fitted with bins and spice drawers and there is a lock on the front as well as on the drawer beneath. This in turn has a smaller drawer within for silver. The rest of the drawer space accommodates a fair quantity of linen. A Kentucky piece, made of cherry, its opalescent glass drawer knobs and short turned legs date it as of the American Empire period, but the valanced outline of the apron is Hepplewhite.

### The American Courting Mirror

Where today a vanity case is one of the many things to be given young women by their suitors, in the eighteenth and early nineteenth centuries small framed mirrors were among the few articles considered proper presents for such circumstances. As such they were called courting mirrors. Furthermore, because of the high cost and relative scarcity of good mirror glass, they were not gifts bought in the penny shop.

These courting glasses were small. Judging by surviving examples, six to eight by ten to twelve inches were the popular sizes. Before America began to trade directly with the treaty ports of China, courting glasses were the careful work of native cabinetmakers. Molded frames, finished with oil or varnish, were of maple, cherry, walnut, or pine. Made mostly in the more sophisticated towns along the Atlantic seaboard, they were simplified examples of the crested mirror frames in vogue from the late Queen Anne years to the start of the Hepplewhite period. Some were without the arched top, but had a well-cut molded frame done in high relief, a simple yet dignified design.

After 1790, when Elias Haskett Derby of Salem, Massachusetts, established direct trade between the Orient and the United States with his ship, *Empress of China,* many courting mirrors were brought back from Canton and other treaty ports. Today they are generally found in the coastal towns of New England. They have frames with finely beaded edges and set with narrow long panels of painted glass inlays. These frames may be of camphor wood, Chinese cherry, teak, or Oriental pine. Some may be lacquer-decorated.

Presumably, many courting glasses were brought home as presents by sailors who had manned ships in the China trade, but a good number were part of the regular cargo. To protect them during the long voyage back, they were each fitted into a small wooden box in which the framed glass was held in place with removable wooden pegs.

In their day, 1790 to about 1830, they were so highly regarded as gifts that many a young woman kept her mirror in its traveling case and hung the choice article on the wall, box and all. With collectors, the boxed examples are the rarest of all, especially if they still retain their original lids. Boxed or not, one of these small glasses makes a colorful and interesting decoration for a guest room, especially as the quality of mirror plate is always high and gives a clear and undistorted reflection, not always found in the larger mirrors of the same date.

About the turn of the nineteenth century American cabinetmakers competed briefly with this China-trade product. The American version (Illustration 20) has a rounded molded frame faced with walnut veneer, varying in tone from dark to light, and an arched top containing a glass panel painted with a conventional design, such as a bird perched on a twig, done in natural colors. The overall dimensions are eight inches wide by a little over thirteen inches high. Carrying the imitation of the Chinese a bit further, some American courting mirrors even had a protecting box.

### The Tabernacle Mirror

The term tabernacle mirror would have been distinct news to looking-glass makers back in 1800 when this type was in style. Both to them and their clients it was a gilt-framed looking glass with classic side columns, corniced top, and decorated upper panel. The present-day name was applied much later and first in England where it was used by furniture designers to designate a niche with an enclosing door, built into a large display piece of furniture where a fine vase or other art object could be shown.

The frames of these particular Sheraton mirrors bore a resemblance to the doors of such niches and so the name "tabernacle" was given them and being distinctive, though inaccurate, it stuck. Gilt frames predominated although mahogany ones were also made. Decorative detail was elaborate if made by a skilled city craftsman, or simple when fashioned by a man working in a country village whose clients preferred them plainer. But the frame was always architectural in design. The upper glass varied. Fine ones were skillfully done with portraits of Washington, landscapes, or scenes from famous naval engagements of the War of 1812, since these mirrors were at the height of popularity

24

during the Napoleonic world upheaval. Simpler tabernacle mirrors had painted glass panels of flower and fruit compositions, crudely enough done to class as American primitive art.

There is such wide variety in these mirrors that their perennial popularity continues today. No matter what kind of furniture one has, urban-sophisticated or country-primitive, a tabernacle mirror can be found to match it. There are a good number still in existence. They were made for a generation or more during the first part of the nineteenth century when mirror-making was at its high point in America and when there were many skilled craftsmen devoted to making home furnishings by hand and after their own individual conceptions of the prevailing styles.

Some of the mirrors have pendent balls decorating the cornice top. They are referred to in England as "Nelson's cannonballs"; in America there has been a fanciful idea that they represent the Thirteen Original Colonies, although examples have been found with considerably more than that number decorating the cornice. It is doubtful if the mirror makers were thinking of any of these things when they made the mirror frames.

Both mirrors illustrated were made by skilled workers. The one with cornice decoration of thirteen pendent balls has a mahogany frame and dates about 1810 (Illustration 21a). It has the characteristic reeded columns of the Sheraton period and the painted decoration of the upper glass is a rather primitively executed landscape. The gilt mirror (Illustration 21b) with double reeded columns and classic molded cornice has a painting in the upper panel of the famous sea fight between the *Constitution* and *Guerrière* which occurred on August 19, 1812. Made between 1815 and 1820, this mirror is signed on the back "Willard & Nolan." They were Boston mirror makers and frame gilders.

### Banjo Clocks by Willard and Others

Inventing and perfecting what is now referred to as a banjo clock was just an incident in a clockmaking career of seventy-seven years. Its inventor, Simon Willard, began making clocks when he was thirteen years old and reluctantly laid down his tools at the age of ninety.

During this long career he made many types of clocks including turret, gallery, church, grandfather or tall case, and the popular banjo which he always referred to as his "patent timepiece." In designing it he probably had in mind the man of moderate means for it was a clear departure from the current tall-case type. The movement was brass, simple but accurate; the case was a practical covering that just happened to resemble a banjo. It was of a form and size that could be hung on a wall and the standard price for it was thirty dollars.

Simon Willard, who was born in Grafton, Massachusetts, in 1753, completed his first experimental banjo clock late in the 1790's. A master craftsman and designer but quite lacking in commercial instinct, he made no effort to patent his timepiece until 1802 when his good friend President Jefferson finally persuaded him to do so.

25

He called his new clock "Improved Patent Timepiece." It caught public favor immediately and his competitors were soon imitating it in spite of the patent. As the only action Willard took against the infringers was to refuse to speak to them, plenty of banjo clocks were produced in shops that were in no way connected with either Simon or his brother Aaron. There were probably thirty or more of the pirating clockmakers on Willard's black list. Among the known ones were David Wood of Newburyport, Reuben Tower of Hingham, William Grant of Boston, Nathaniel Monroe and Samuel Whiting of Concord, and Zaccheus Gates of Charlestown.

None of them equalled Willard in craftsmanship or quality of design. He made four thousand of his "patent timepieces." All were finely proportioned and were of the best materials and finest workmanship. The example in Illustration 22 is typical, with its acorn finial, molded bracket beneath the pendulum box, brass "side boys" flanking the flaring neck, and simple decoration on the oblong pendulum box with the inscription "S. Willard's Patent."

His brother Aaron also made excellent banjo clocks, often more ornate in decoration, especially that of the pendulum door where a scenic pattern was favored. Simon's were without such pictorial effects and also eschewed the spread eagle as a finial motif.

Banjo cases and decoration varied, according to individual makers. One elaborate variation was the lyre clock, designed by Aaron Willard, Jr., a few years before he took over his father's prosperous clock business on Washington Street, Boston, when the latter retired in 1823. The Directoire furniture style was in high favor and one of its decorative details was the lyre motif which, with acanthus carving, was much used by Duncan Phyfe. Young Willard took the lyre motif and used it in a new case design for his uncle's timepiece. It was elaborate enough for the passing fashion but still possessed artistic merit. The work of making such cases of course went to local mirror and picture frame craftsmen who were experts in carving, gilding, and other ornamental details.

A good timekeeper in a handsome case, the lyre clock was well received and many were produced by the Willard family and other Massachusetts clockmakers between 1815 and 1840. These other makers were either former apprentices of the Willards or lived in nearby towns and were familiar with their methods. A good example is an early lyre clock made in Boston before 1820 which bears on its dial the name of "Sawin & Dyer," (Illustration 23). The case is typical of the best made in this variation of the banjo. It is of mahogany. The lyre-shaped front is decorated with acanthus leaf carving and frames a glass panel painted to simulate the strings of the instrument. The pendulum box has an oblong door with a panel of mirror glass. An eagle, favored ornament of the day, appears as the finial.

Sawin and Dyer were partners from 1800 to 1820. Sawin had been trained in the shop of the elder Aaron Willard, was considered a fine clockmaker and often commissioned by the Willards to make clocks for them. Dyer, who was also a maker of banjo-clock movements, left Boston in 1820 and later settled in Middlebury, Vermont, where he continued as a clockmaker for some years. Sawin worked in Boston until 1863. His shop was at 33 Cornhill where, according to his advertisements, he was a "Manufacturer of all kinds of clocks for Church, Gallery, Bank, Office, Factory; Watchclocks and common House Clocks."

### *The Popular Pillar-and-Scroll Clock*

The appearance of a package frequently is the key to its success or failure. Eli Terry discovered this when he began making wooden-works shelf clocks in quantity. Since the primary purpose of a clock is to tell time accurately, he had seen to it that his thirty-hour wood-movement could do that and could also be produced at a price within reach of the many clock-less households.

At first he put his new clock in a plain but well-proportioned box case. It would be inaccurate to assume that this plain package was without takers in a day when inexpensive timepieces were in demand. But from it evolved an ornamental case which Terry named his "pillar-and-scroll." A handsome clock with the neat proportions of the earlier box case but with Sheraton details added, such as the valanced bracket base, the slender colonnettes or pillars, and scrolled pediment usually with brass urn finials, it was popular from the start.

It sold for only fifteen dollars and, although money was scarce after the War of 1812, demand was so great that Seth Thomas paid Terry a thousand dollars for a license to make this type of clock. The arrangement was apparently profitable, for each man made a profit of six thousand dollars the first year. Other clockmakers pirated the design without shame and without the courtesy of a license, especially those in and around Plymouth, Connecticut. Patents were seemingly made to be infringed on in the early nineteenth century. An exception to this was Silas Hoadley, an early partner of Terry and Thomas. He showed considerable originality in movement design and so did not infringe on Terry's patent. A number of his pillar-and-scroll clocks are known as Franklin clocks because of the label, "Time Is Money, Franklin: Clocks with improvement of Burling Pivots."

With so many clockmakers producing this type of shelf clock, technical variations in the wooden movement and in case decoration resulted. Terry also continued to experiment. With his earlier pillar-and-scrolls, for instance, the escapement wheel is outside the dial. With the clock in Illustration 24, made about 1820, it is inside and therefore not visible.

The pillar-and-scroll clock stayed in fashion for about twenty-five years. Its largest production was in the Naugatuck Valley of Connecticut. Massachusetts had a less pleasing version with an American Empire flavor. There was also a Pennsylvania variation which housed an eight-day cast brass movement. These were made from about 1820 to 1830.

Because these clocks were made in quantity and in an era when good workmanship was the rule, quite a number in running condition are still extant. They are deservedly popular now with those who want a beautiful old clock to go with their heirlooms. If such a clock has Eli Terry's label and the painted glass in the lower half of the glazed door is original, it is worth many times the price asked by its originator. Of course, one with a Seth Thomas label is not to be passed up, nor those of other makers who pirated the model and were able craftsmen who recognized a good design and, according to the easy-going custom of the time, copied it.

### *Chauncey Jerome and His Clock*

The Jerome stamped-brass clock was the fruit of a business depression— the Panic of 1837. It was the result of a frenzied casting about for a product that could be made and sold for a price low enough for the public to buy. The Terry wooden-movement timepieces had been the popular and moderately priced clocks for a quarter of a century but not only were they now beyond the reach of the average citizen but their wooden mechanisms were apt to be affected adversely by the weather.

Chauncey Jerome (1793-1860) was a former employee of Eli Terry, making clock cases. In the 1820's he had formed a partnership with his brother Noble, an excellent movement maker, and Elijah Darrow. They produced wooden-works clocks, along with other Connecticut craftsmen, including a "looking glass" type that was very popular until the bad year of 1837.

With many of these clocks still in stock and realizing that they would not sell, Jerome got the idea of a cheaper movement of stamped brass. His brother Noble went to work on it and perfected the movement in a short time. Inexpensive, accurate, and dependable, it at once superseded the temperamental wooden-works clock, made a fortune for its inventor and put a clock in every household that had three dollars to spare. The case was purely functional. Box-like, its front had the ogee molding in crotch-grain mahogany veneer of the current American Empire style. It framed a two-glassed paneled door, the upper part plain glass to protect the dial; the lower one decorated with a painted design, either floral or pictorial.

The clock in Illustration 25 is of the type patented by Jerome and has a label on the inside of the door which reads: "J. J. & Beals Clock Establishment, Corner of Hanover and Blackstone Streets, also at 422 Washington Street, Boston." This firm was listed at these locations in the Boston Directory only in 1846. They were probably dealers rather than clockmakers. The painted decoration was a popular one at the time and is of historic interest now.

"Croton Fountain" in New York's City Hall park was a visible sign of the city's much improved water supply, with two reservoirs, one in what is now Central Park and the other where the Public Library at Fifth Avenue and 42nd Street now stands. Completed in 1842, it took the place of the dug wells, springs, and ponds on which New York City had previously depended.

The Jerome clocks still keep good time and, while they bring a price many times their original one, are among the moderately inexpensive antiques. Those with the ogee case are earlier and more desirable than the steeple type which came in with the Victorian years.

28

## A Victorian Parlor Set

In the Victorian period, custom furniture shops and factories often made furniture in sets—parlor, dining room, and bedroom. The number of pieces in a parlor set ranged from a sofa, armchair, a lady chair with the low small arms that hoop skirts required, and four side chairs, to the more extensive kind that included a matching center table with a cartouche-shaped white marble top, an ottoman of the same height and size as the seat of the large armchair, a whatnot, and small slant-front desk.

It is rather unusual to find one of these sets complete today. But anyone who has a sofa and armchair or other pieces and wants to complete it, can do so. Victorian furniture is still plentiful enough so that patience and repeated visits to antique shops in one's vicinity will, in time, result in the other matching pieces at moderate prices.

The parlor set in Illustration 26 is typical of American factory-made work between 1860 and 1875. Its design sources are French, inspired by those of the Louis XV period and revived by Louis Philippe who occupied the French throne from 1830 to 1848. Some of the furniture was simple and restrained in design like this parlor set; some was heavily laden with carving in the form of bunches of grapes and leaves or flowers and foliage. As a rule the pieces with less ornate design are earlier. The sofa in this set is of the medallion-back type. All of the pieces have the French type of cabriole leg as well as the continuous grooved molding, known as "finger molding," in their framework.

Haircloth was the original upholstery of about ninety percent of the early Victorian furniture made in the United States. There was nothing like it for long wear, as is demonstrated by the number of pieces still to be found with original upholstery in fair to good condition. But there is no denying that it is funereal, slippery, and prickly.

Therefore, for present day use, the most effective material for re-upholstering such pieces is a satin in a plain color, preferably red or old gold. It is a good idea also to omit the tufting of the backs since it creates a fussy appearance. The same can be said for upholstery material with a figured pattern. The curves and carvings of the walnut framework provide design enough.

## John Henry Belter and His Rosewood Furniture

About the time that Duncan Phyfe closed his large shop on Fulton Street after half a century as New York's leading cabinetmaker, a young man working in a new furniture style established a shop at 40 Chatham Square. He was John Henry Belter, recently arrived from Germany and excellently trained in cabinetmaking and wood carving.

Phyfe had used mahogany and occasionally satinwood. Belter worked only in rosewood and what he made was done in an adaptation of the French Louis XV style, now known as Early Victorian. Where Phyfe's genius had been for supremely fine workmanship, inspired by the furniture designs of Hepplewhite and Sheraton, Belter originated a method of laminating rosewood which made it possible for him to create a unique style of handsomely carved and pierced chairs with concave backs.

29

The furniture for which he is best known is his drawing room suites which he made for wealthy New Yorkers from 1844 until his death in 1865. Examples that remain range from a set consisting of a sofa, armchair, lady chair and two or four side chairs to one comprised of two matching sofas or love seats, two armchairs, two lady chairs, six side chairs, an ottoman, a child's chair and a center table with oval cartouche-shaped top. All are elaborately carved and, like the chairs in Illustration 27, have the finger-molded cabriole legs characteristic of the Victorian style.

The distinctive design and workmanship of Belter can be seen in his chair-backs which are always of laminated construction, that is, thin layers of rosewood glued together and varying from six to eight in number. These backs are concave and beautifully shaped in an outline of balancing scrolls with a crested top, either rose or shell carved. For his arm and lady chairs, he used a central upholstered panel framed by a border of carved and pierced rosewood, done in full-blown and bud roses, foliage, and scroll motifs.

For side chair backs, he used either a central upholstered panel or one of carved and pierced wood in which flowers, foliage, bunches of grapes were framed by interlacing scrollwork. The reverse of all Belter chair-backs were always faced with plain rosewood (Illustration 28).

After a few years Belter moved from Chatham Square. He first located his shop at 327 Broadway; then in 1855 he moved to larger quarters at 1222 Third Avenue where he remained until his death. He worked closely with the founder of the Steinway piano firm and devised for him the method of laminating the rounded front corners of square piano cases and designed the heavy cabriole legs needed to support the weight of these instruments. He kept his method of laminating wood a secret for many years but finally took out a patent for it in 1858. He died five years later and, just before that, made quite sure that his designs and methods would stop with him by destroying his patterns and smashing his pattern molds.

Always expensive, made in limited quantity and that ceasing with the death of its originator, Belter furniture is scarce today and correspondingly costly. The lace-like and deeply-cut carving was the work of carvers trained in Alsace-Lorraine or the Black Forest of Germany. He considered men from these regions the most proficient and would have no others.

### The Grecian Couch, Victorian Style

What the day-bed had been to the William and Mary, Queen Anne, and Chippendale periods, the couch was from the Sheraton through the Victorian years. The difference was that the day-bed was an ample side chair with seat extended to six feet; the couch was a modified sofa with a half back and one raised end.

The day-bed was sturdy, designed primarily for masculine use; the couch was of dainty design, usually with curved lines. How partial women were to it is indicated by book and magazine illustrations of the period showing elegantly clad ladies circumspectly reclining on a couch like the one in Illustration 29. In a deluxe edition of *Uncle Tom's Cabin*, published in 1853, there is a half-page chapter heading showing Mr. and Mrs. St. Clare on the veranda of their luxurious Louisiana plantation. He is enjoying his after-dinner cigar; she is half reclining on a couch with high arched head-rest. Her voluminous hoop skirt is draped to conceal both ankles and feet.

This type of couch, a Victorian version of Sheraton's Grecian design, attained such popularity that elaborate parlor suites sometimes included a matching pair, one with raised end at the right and the other at the left. They were so designed that they could be placed in balancing positions on either side of a marble-manteled fireplace.

The couch illustrated was made by John Henry Belter, famous for his elaborate rosewood drawing room furniture, and may have been part of such a suite. Several of them are still in existence intact. This Belter couch is an impressive piece, six feet long and twenty-eight inches wide. The arched headpiece that shows its day-bed ancestry is joined at the front to a low enclosed arm and at the rear sweeps down in an undulating curve that almost reaches the open right end. A carved and pierced full-length cresting surmounts it. Its design is typically Belter and consists of intertwined tendrils and cyma-curved scrolls combined with leafage, bunches of grapes, and at the top of the arching, a medallion of roses in bloom carved in high relief.

Exposed parts of the frame are finger-molded, with the front seat rail slightly valanced and decorated with carved conventionalized leafage scrolls. The four short cabriole legs have finger molding and flower-carved knees and end in rudimentary feet fitted with socket casters.

Less elaborate couches with the same general outline were made for use in a lady's boudoir or bedroom. Still others with variations in detail were made for parlors of pretentious homes. Since many of them are both comfortable and practical pieces of furniture, they are now regaining some of their original popularity.

### Spool-Turned Furniture

The Victorian style reflected a variety of influences—the designs of Louis XV, the Gothic, and the Renaissance. This hybrid reached America by way of England about 1850 where it was quickly adapted to public taste. An American contribution to it was the ornamental detail known as spool-turning.

Taking its name from its resemblance to a series of spools placed end to end, it replaced the baluster-shaped turnings that had been in favor for nearly two centuries with furniture of the less pretentious sort. Consequently spool-turnings are apt to appear on pieces of the American cottage type but are not a dominant characteristic of contemporary English and Continental furniture.

It is an American detail and the reason for it lies in power-driven lathes for wood turning. These were developed by ingenious Yankees, beginning about 1820. Before that, turned parts were done on a lathe driven by a foot treadle. Slow and strenuous, even with the twelve-hour working day then current, it could not cope with the needs of the small furniture factories that were springing up and gradually forcing cabinetmaking shops to close. So the Victorian furniture makers in the 1850's turned to the larger power-driven lathes devised by Yankees like Thomas Blanchard of Massachusetts.

Here the turner had only to concern himself with guiding his cutting chisels. With water or steam power to do the rest, not only was the work done more quickly but the details of spool-turning called for less exact work than the earlier baluster design.

This spool-turned cottage furniture came into fashion about 1840 and continued into the 1880's. A familiar part of home furnishings between 1840 and 1865 was the low-post spool bed. Sometimes referred to as a "Jenny Lind" bed because it was in fashion at the time of her American concert tours, the early ones had four low posts with headboards and footboards either solid or constructed of short slender spindles turned to match the posts.

Much less numerous and contained within a special area was its close relative, the tall-post spool bed (Illustration 30). Structurally, the main difference was one of height. The posts were from five and one-half to seven feet tall and either surmounted by a full-size tester or knob-turned finials. The parts were sometimes turned in other than spool-shaped units. With minor variations they ranged through bobbin, knob, sausage, vase-and-ring to a large plain ring-turning or that of two balls separated by a thin ring element. Which design unit was used was a small matter since all such lathe work went under the generic term of spool-turning.

The material was turned in large diameter for posts and rails and in small diameter for spindles, and a bed could be assembled readily by cutting off the required parts from the longer lengths of turnings as they came from the lathe. Beds like the one illustrated are mostly found in long established homes in the Middle West and as far south as Mississippi. They turn up with enough regularity in antique shops located in this area to indicate that they were popular in the region when they were new. This bed is part of the furnishings of the Hercules Dousman house, Villa Louis, at Prairie duChien, Wisconsin, now maintained as a museum under the sponsorship of the Wisconsin Historical Society.

Tall-post spool beds were made from 1850 to 1865 of black walnut in the full-size, in single size, in child's and crib sizes. Several present-day furniture factories have now revived the style, but copies can be easily recognized by the posts which are much slenderer, not over two and one-half inches in diameter, as against three to four inches with the originals.

Along with the spool bed, room sets with matching details were developed so the list of spool pieces includes tables, chairs, bureaus with attached mirrors, desks, especially those of the schoolmaster type, settees, whatnots, music stands, dressing glasses, and towel racks.

With pieces like the dressing table (Illustration 31), the legs were always spool-turned as were the spindles of chair backs. For small pieces, such as a mirror frame and supports on a dressing glass, spool-turning was largely used as applied ornament. Legs on chests of drawers were spool-turned as might be the cresting of backboards. Spool-turned supports of an attached mirror usually ended in urn-shaped finials. For such turnings a strong close-grained wood was necessary so spool pieces were usually of maple, birch, black walnut, and sometimes cherry. Pieces made of the latter are quite unusual.

*(Illustration 17)* **A Pennsylvania Dutch Water Bench, made of pine between 1830 and 1850. The center shelf is unusual and possibly a later addition.**

*(Illustration 18)* **An Early Nineteenth-century Southern Hunt Board of Walnut.**

*(Illustration 19)* Sugar Chest from a Kentucky Plantation. Made of cherry. The opalescent glass knobs on the drawer front and the turning of the legs are American Empire details, dating this piece about 1820-1830.

*(Illustration 20)* **An American Courting Mirror, ca. 1800. The rounded molded frame is of veneered walnut. Above is a glass panel primitively painted with bird perched on a twig.**

*(Illustration 21a)* Tabernacle Mirror with Mahogany Frame. Made ca. 1810.

*(Illustration 21b)* Tabernacle Mirror with Architectural Gilt Frame. The engagement between the *Constitution* and the *Guerrière* is depicted in the upper painted glass panel. Made by Willard & Nolan, Boston, ca. 1815-1820.

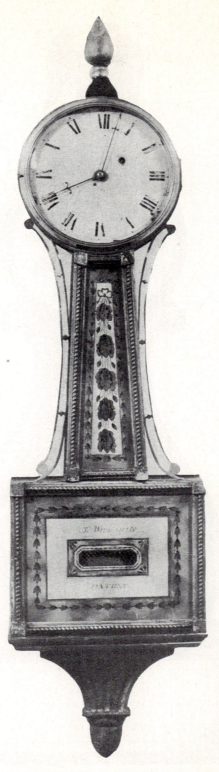

*(Illustration 22)* **Early Willard Banjo Clock.**

*(Illustration 23)* Lyre Clock, a Later Form of the Banjo.

*(Illustration 24)* **An Eli Terry Pillar-and-Scroll Clock. Ca. 1820.**

*(Illustration 25)* A Chauncey Jerome Clock with Stamped Brass Movement.

*(Illustration 26)* Typical Victorian Black-Walnut Parlor Set. Sofa, gentleman's armchair, lady chair, and four side chairs retaining original black haircloth upholstery.

*(Illustration 27)* Characteristic Belter Chairs with Elaborately Carved Backs.

*(Illustration 28) Nine-Piece Belter Drawing Room Suite.*

*(Illustration 29)* Elaborate Victorian Couch Made by Belter.

*(Illustration 30)* **Tall-Post Spool Bed of Black Walnut.**

*(Illustration 31)* **Spool-Turned Dressing Table Made of Bird's-Eye, Curly, and Plain Maple.**

*(Illustration 32)* **A Victorian Ottoman of Rosewood in the French Style.**

*(Illustration 33)* **Mid-Western Food Safe, ca. 1850. Its eighteen pierced tin panels are set into a painted wood framing.**

*(Illustration 34)* Liverpool Pitcher with American Ship and United States Arms
Decoration in Black, ca. 1804.

*(Illustration 35)* **Commodore Perry's Victory on Large Staffordshire Pitcher, ca. 1815-1820.**

(*Illustration 36*) Top, "Capitol at Washington" Platter, ca. 1830. Below, left and right, Philadelphia Water Works plates and, center, a Chain of States plate.

(*Illustration 37*) Above, "Landing of Lafayette" Platter, ca. 1825.

(*Illustration 38*) Below, "Sandusky, Ohio" Platter, ca. 1835.

*(Illustration 40)* Above, Bennington Reclining-Doe Flower-Holder, dated 1849.

*(Illustration 39)* Below, Rockingham Houndhandled Pitchers.

*(Illustration 41)* **Early Staffordshire Salt-Glaze Tureen, ca. 1750.**

*(Illustration 42)* Staffordshire Salt-Glaze Plate with Embossed Polychrome Decoration, ca. 1760.

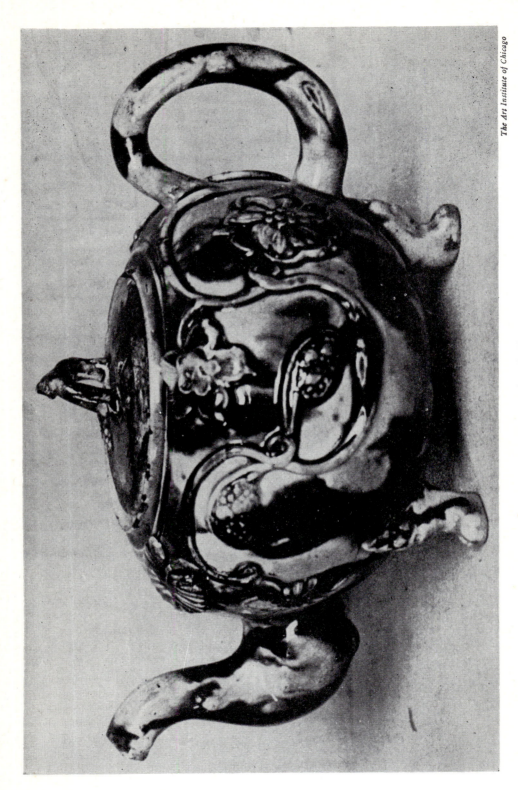

*(Illustration 43)* Whieldon Tortoise-Shell Teapot, ca. 1760.

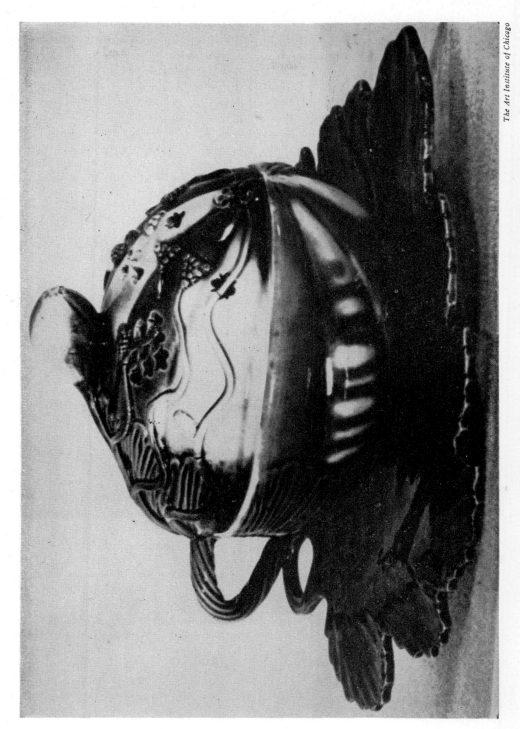

*(Illustration 44)* Wedgwood Dish in Form of Melon, with Cauliflower Glaze.

*(Illustration 45)* Wedgwood Jasperware Plate, with Characteristic Dark Blue Background.

*(Illustration 46a)* "Dance of the Hours" Vase in Wedgwood Jasperware, Modeled by Hackwood.

*(Illustration 46b)* **Wine Pitcher in Wedgwood Jasperware, Modeled by Flaxman.**

*(Illustration* 47) **A Variety of English Copper Lustre, ca. 1820-1835.**

*(Illustration 48)* **A Silver Resist Tea Set, Staffordshire, ca. 1810.**

*(Illustration 49)* "Sir Isaac Newton," by Ralph Wood II, ca. 1790.

### The Ottoman, A Victorian Furniture Form

As the name indicates, this auxiliary seat for a Victorian parlor set was inspired by a Turkish pile of small rugs used as a low seat. From its usage it could well be considered the effete descendant of the austere joined stool of the seventeenth century which was accepted as a fitting seat for "women, children, and lesser folk." Two centuries later, the well-behaved young person was expected to choose the upholstered but back-less ottoman as a proper seat in the presence of elders.

This piece of furniture dates from a little before the beginning of the Victorian period and remained in favor through the end of the century. Since this period included not one but eight sub-styles, the types of ottomans naturally varied with the chair fashions they matched. The high point came with the French Louis XV sub-style when the ottoman with slender cabriole legs was a standard unit of many matching parlor sets.

The one in Illustration 32 is a typical example of that period and when used with its companion armchair the two pieces become a sort of chaise longue. The French-style ottoman and large or "gentleman's" armchair are of corresponding size and the ottoman has an upholstered seat, crowning, and is equipped with springs like that of its matching armchair. It is the same height from the floor. Seat rails are serpentined, finger-molded, and ornamented with central medallions of carved flowers or fruits, flanked by leafage done in low or medium relief. There usually is carving also on the knees of the four cabriole legs. Black walnut was the usual wood but rosewood was also fashionable, especially for expensive, cabinetmaker-produced furniture.

This type of ottoman was made in quantity by furniture factories and manufacturers of sofa and chair frames from about 1850 to 1865. Some were made with longer legs and used as dressing table seats or as piano stools. The chair-high ottoman is desirable in this style and more apt to be found as a separate piece today than as part of a set.

Ottomans in other Victorian sub-styles include the spool-turned which was being made at the same time. This has plain straight rails and is supported by four spool-turned legs of either black walnut or walnut-stained native hard wood.

There is also the bracket-foot type which bears traces of the earlier American Empire period in that it has a rectangular base with either an ogee-molded or serpentined skirt veneered in crotch-grain mahogany and four low bracket feet fitted with casters. It is sometimes as large as a love seat and dates from about 1840 to 1855.

Later and less desirable is the lyre-trestle ottoman which dates from 1850 to 1875 and is supported by a pair of open lyre-shaped trestles braced by a stretcher.

### The Mid-Western Food Safe

An early nineteenth-century piece of kitchen furniture which has been adapted for use in the modern home is a wooden cupboard with perforated tin panels in doors and sides. Known as a safe throughout the Middle West and parts of the South, where it was popular from the early 1800's to as late as 1870, it was originally used for storing food.

33

In its simple outline, the stile and rail construction of the seventeenth century can be seen, but in place of carved or plain wooden panels, those of pierced tin in ornate design served the double purpose of letting in air and keeping out mice and flies. Like the present day refrigerator, it was a repository for leftovers as well as cured and cooked meats, pastries, milk, and other foods.

Sometimes these safes were devoted entirely to pans of milk and were placed in the cellar or some other cool place: sometimes they held the weekly baking of bread, cake, and pies; still another use was for the keeping of vegetables and fruit which also benefited by the moderate circulation of air. The perforated tin panels were the forerunners of screening since the only thing resembling it at the time was a netting composed of horse hair and cotton thread which was used in sieves.

Native woods, both soft and hard, were used for the framework and the three or more shelves of the interior. Most of the safes were simply cupboards resting on four turned legs. A few were made with two long drawers with wooden fronts placed above the cupboard. I have also seen an occasional safe built on the chest-on-chest idea. Cherry, walnut, poplar, pine, and other woods used were either left natural or painted in dark shades of red, green, blue, or brown.

The perforated tin panels were not only decorative but the idea of them went back to the fourteenth century when pierced metal lanterns first appeared in Europe. The earliest of these were of brass or copper; then came those of sheet iron or tin. The Thirteen Colonies were well established before much tin was used in America, but when, in the early nineteenth century, there was work for the tinsmith, one of his jobs was designing and stamping tin sheets in intricate patterns for use in lanterns and foot stoves.

He began by cutting the tin sheets to the proper size. These he laid on a bed of lead, sand, soft wood, or other suitable substance. Then he traced his pattern, put his dies in position and struck them with a hammer, piercing the tin along the lines of the design. The latter was elaborate and varied, with half moon, rising sun, cathedral, and sunburst among the most favored themes.

Pierced designs in old food safes showed even greater variety. Some had the rising sun motif (Illustration 33); others had an urn and floral pattern. Both the heart motif and that of the six-pointed star indicated Pennsylvania Dutch inspiration. In fact, it is generally believed that these ingenious food safes originated in the area occupied by those emigrants from the Counties Palatine where the pierced tinwork was undoubtedly well known.

Today it is the beauty of the pierced tinwork that makes them so desirable. The earliest and best were made according to old cabinetmaking ways, with uprights and horizontal members of the framework fitted together with mortice-and-tenon joints. Now the food safes no longer stand in the kitchen but, cleaned and refinished, have other uses. Collectors of such primitive items as wooden cooking utensils and implements, powder horns, or early slipware dishes find them excellent cabinets for their treasures. Some people like them as cupboards for bed linen. They also fit well in a game room. I once saw one so used in Iowa. The cupboard made a convenient wine cellar and, as the safe was only four feet high, the owner used the top as a bar.

34

# II

# China

## *Early Souvenir Pitchers*

L IVERPOOL PITCHERS, with their neat black decoration, take their name from the famous English seaport from where so many of these pitchers were brought home to America by returning sailors.

The black transfer-printed design marked a revolution in earthenware decoration and made it possible for average people to have attractive dishes on their tables. Transfer printing was just what the name indicates. A copperplate engraving was coated with a special ink, a sheet of paper was pressed on the inked plate and, while still wet, transferred to the unglazed ceramic surface. Firing and glazing followed. This process was first commercialized in Liverpool by John Sadler and Guy Green, in 1756.

This decorative china made Liverpool and Staffordshire potteries famous all over the world, and especially in America. Josiah Wedgwood brought the cream ware on which the transfer designs were printed to a high state of development and, in 1763, named in "queen's ware" in honor of Queen Charlotte. He sent this ware over thirty miles by cart to Sadler and Green for its black printed decoration. Similar cream ware was also made in Bristol, Leeds, Sunderland, and Liverpool. Typical of the latter place were a slightly grayer tone and heavier quality than the true Wedgwood. Of the potters making it in Liverpool, only two consistently marked their wares. They were Herculaneum Pottery and Richard Hall & Sons.

Liverpool pitchers with black decoration were in favor until about 1815 when they were superseded by those with transfer printing in color, such as the well-known blue and white. During the period of black and white, pieces intended to catch the eye of a seafaring man included pitchers, mugs, plates, handleless cups and saucers, and even a punch bowl, a favorite present for the

35

captain to bring back to the owners of his ship. Pitchers were the most popular and the designs were as varied as the tastes of the buyers. The stock design was a ship. With a few touches, it easily became a souvenir of the voyage. The flag that flew at the mast was added by hand. Under the spout there was usually a design where the names of buyer and recipient could be added and the whole given additional firing.

Other popular designs were those with a Washington motif—a bust of the great man or a representation of his tomb. The coat of arms of the United States was another patriotic touch (Illustration 34). This particular pitcher was made for an American sea captain. The black decoration includes a three-masted ship flying the American flag and, under the spout, the coat of arms of the United States with thirteen stars above. Below is the inscription: "Peace, Commerce and honest Friendship with all Nations. Entangling Alliances with none. Anno Domini 1804." The latter reflects the hopeful attitude of the time when the aim of the United States was to keep clear of the Napoleonic conflict.

That this aim was not realized is reflected by the quantities of Staffordshire pottery flowing across the Atlantic after the War of 1812. Decorated expressly for the American trade, this ware often showed such scenes as English and American ships in combat on Lake Champlain.

Such china appeared in well-established homes along the eastern seacoast, rolled westward in covered wagons, and formed part of the cargo on the Mississippi River boats. Especially desired by the buying public was a good-sized pitcher with a colorful decoration of copper lustre bands and stripes which set off a transfer-printed picture of a naval battle, entitled "Second View of Com. Perry's Victory" (Illustration 35). It is one of two views of this famous naval engagement which took place on September 10, 1813. During the course of the battle, Perry's flagship was lost to the British, but he transferred to another ship, the *Niagara*, and gained the victory. The two views show the fifteen ships engaged in somewhat different formation.

Both were taken from paintings done by the artist Michele Felice Corne (1752-1832), who was born in Italy, came to America and settled, first in Salem, Massachusetts, and later in Boston. He also painted a naval scene with the *Constitution* in close action with the *Guerrière*. Engravings of these three paintings were published by Abel Brown of Boston in 1816. In due time, they came into the hands of the Staffordshire potters along with many others that provided subjects for the American market.

### Staffordshire China for Americans

Americans had been partial to the products of that area in central England known as "The Potteries" for three-quarters of a century when, about 1820, china decorated with American scenic designs began to be exported to the United States. This ware, now called "Historic Blue and White," quickly caught the fancy of the citizens of the new republic and demand increased until by 1825, more Staffordshire china was arriving here monthly than had come over in a year during the 1790's when the great Josiah Wedgwood's wares were at their height

This transfer-decorated earthenware was usually patterned in a deep blue, although six or eight other colors were occasionally used. The designs numbered almost 700 and were used by thirty or more Staffordshire potters. These designs were not hard to come by since American artists were finding excellent material for their canvases in the scenic views of America. These in turn were often reproduced as prints or magazine illustrations and were readily accessible to the Staffordshire potters.

The dishes which resulted were handsome, inexpensive, and appealed to patriotism and civic pride. Naturally, dinner services, tea sets, and other combinations were in demand. Typical examples of these dishes are a platter and three plates (Illustration 36). The platter has a border of medallions of roses with leafage repeated twelve times. It frames a view of the Capitol at Washington taken from a print published in 1831. This design was used by several potters who often varied the details. This particular platter bears the mark of J. & W. Ridgway, sons of Job Ridgway who started a pottery at Hanley in 1790. Design variations include the two figures in the foreground on horseback and the tall tree with odd foliage which these potters so much favored as to make it almost an additional mark. They were also partial to views of buildings rather than natural scenery.

The plates illustrated below, right and left, are examples of the same scene with variations. It is of the Philadelphia water works and dam, drawn by Thomas Birch and published by Edward Parker in 1824. In the plate at left, by an unknown potter, there is a steamboat in the foreground; the one on the right has a barge with oarsmen and in the immediate foreground two figures and a tall tree. This plate bears the imprint of Joseph Stubbs who had a pottery at Burslem from 1790 to 1829. He also produced views of Boston, New York, and New Jersey.

One of the best known and most popular designs appears on the central plate which is part of a dinner service. It is the Chain of States, so called from its border which has the names of fifteen states on ribbon loops with a star between each. The scenes in the center are varied and relatively unimportant. Framing each is an inner border showing a portrait of Washington, a figure of America blindfolded, and one of Independence kneeling. This handsome pattern was produced by James and Ralph Clews of Cobridge, working from 1819 to 1836.

Another popular and famous pattern produced by this firm was one showing the landing of Lafayette on his farewell tour of 1824 (Illustration 37). General Lafayette's visit to America gave the young republic, whose states then numbered twenty-four, its first chance to show what it could do in entertaining an honored guest. He arrived in New York in August and stayed thirteen months during which he was feted everywhere on a nation-wide tour. A natural product of this patriotic fervor was a liberal supply of souvenir items.

Among them were the blue and white transfer-decorated dishes from Staffordshire. The Clews brothers took the most popular print of the visit and produced a dinner service for the American trade. The print, bearing the title "Landing of Gen. Lafayette at Castle Garden, New York, 16th August, 1824," was made by Samuel Maverick, New York printer, engraver, and early nineteenth-century forerunner of the modern news photographer.

The print appeared on each dish of the Clews dinner services surrounded by a border of large and small flower clusters. Maverick portrayed the event realistically and with commendable detail. Lafayette's ship *Cadmus,* escorted by the three-masted ships *Robert Fulton* and *Chancellor Livingston,* is shown approaching Castle Garden, then connected with the mainland by a foot bridge. The American flag with twenty-four stars is unfurled in the breeze and, in the foreground, smoke from a welcoming salute of six cannon is plainly visible. Castle Garden was originally built as a fort on a rock formation. Later, as the narrow channel separating it from the mainland filled in, it became part of Battery Park where it was used as a recreation hall for three generations and then as an aquarium.

Although a great number of the Clews dinner services were sold in America, because of the soft earthenware and frequent use, breakage over the years was heavy. The owner of even one piece now is fortunate. Platters are especially desirable. They occur in two sizes, 19 by 14¾ inches and 15½ by 12 inches. Clews' usual mark was a crown surrounded by the words "Clews' Warranted Staffordshire." Some pieces also have an importer's mark, "J. Greenfield's China Store, No. 77 Pearl Street, New York."

The earliest scenic dishes showed pictures of long-established towns in the east, but as pioneer settlements of the Middle West grew into cities and towns, views of them appeared, found their way to Staffordshire, and came back on blue and white transfer ware. Most of these views were used by potters who failed to mark their pieces except for the name of the view which was usually surrounded by a wreath of leaves and flowers (Illustration 38). This platter shows a view of Sandusky, Ohio, settled in 1817 and well established by 1840 as indicated by this view, done by an unknown artist.

Other western views used by anonymous potters were Detroit, Michigan, Chillicothe and Columbus, Ohio, Vevey, Indiana, and Louisville, Kentucky. Among the known potters who used western views, J. & J. Jackson produced some light blue and white ware decorated with a picture of White Sulphur Springs, Delaware, Ohio. Ralph Stevenson and Enoch Wood used a view drawn by Captain Basil Hall about 1828, "Shipping Port on the Ohio in Kentucky." This port was located about two miles below Louisville. Enoch Wood also used two views of Transylvania University, Lexington, Kentucky.

Historic Staffordshire ware with western views is in demand today because it is attractive, rare, and shows the cities and towns as they looked a century and more ago. Some of the views are to be found nowhere else but on these dishes which were once so plentiful. The Sandusky, Ohio, view is one of the views most eagerly sought after. Originally it must have been made as regular tableware, but now even examples in the form of platters are rare and bring as much as $500.

### Rockingham Houndhandle Pitchers

The American Pottery Company in Jersey City, New Jersey, was the first to make Rockingham ware in the United States. The original creation of this ware, with its rich brown glaze and mottled pattern, was in England where it was first perfected about 1780 in Yorkshire. It was named for the Marquis of Rockingham on whose estate the pottery was located.

The most familiar of the Rockingham pieces were teapots. They were soon in wide use in England and America because they were attractive, durable, and inexpensive. Pitchers were probably next in favor and they ranged in capacity from a little over a pint to two-and-a-half quarts. They also lent themselves to decorative effects on handle, spout, and body. The production of Rockingham teapots and pitchers soon spread beyond Yorkshire to the Staffordshire potters who exported them in large numbers to America.

Among the designs in pitchers was a hunting motif on the body in high relief, with handle modeled in the shape of a hound. Demand for this type, as well as other items of Rockingham ware, increased during the early nineteenth century until, in 1840, the American Pottery Company asked Daniel Greatback, a designer and potter in the employ of John and William Ridgway of Stafford-shire, to come to Jersey City. He stayed with this company until 1852, designing pitchers of varying sizes and patterns that are now collector's items. From Jersey City he moved to Bennington, Vermont, and then to East Liverpool, Ohio, where he continued as the leading designer of this ware.

His designs, especially of houndhandle pitchers, were copied by other potteries and made in many localities, from southern Vermont to Ohio. There were probably about twenty potteries producing them. Although they were popular and plentiful in their day, the houndhandle pitcher was in every-day use and consequently is now a rare item, desirable because of its modeling and decoration.

The six examples in Illustration 39 were all made in the United States. The one at top left was produced between 1849 and 1854. It is marked A. Cadmus Congress Pottery, South Amboy, N. J. Next to it is a smaller pitcher in a deep brown glaze with a hunting scene in a lighter color. It was made in the 1850's by William E. Warner, West Troy, N. Y. The pitcher at the right of it has a bird-hunting scene on the opposite side and, on the side shown, two birds in trees. The hunting scene includes a hunter taking aim, his dog at his side.

The pitcher in the bottom row, left, is richly colored and has a relief decoration of a hunting scene showing a hunter with dog pursuing a running stag. The houndhandle is unusually large. The small pitcher next to it was made in Baltimore, Maryland, at the pottery of Edwin Bennett. It has a handsome mask spout, a houndhandle, and flower, rabbit, and bird decorations in relief. Lastly, the pitcher at the lower right is a beautiful example in every detail, with houndhandle realistically modeled. It bears the mark "Rookville Works, Pottsville Schy'l Co. Penna."

### Rockingham Animal Figures from Bennington

Bennington and Rockingham ware are practically synonymous in the minds of many collectors. Rockingham ware, as described in the preceding section, originated in Yorkshire, England, on the estate of Charles, Marquis of Rockingham, and was first made in America about 1840 by the Jersey City Pottery Company.

Eight years later, a short-lived venture, known first as Lyman and Fenton and shortly afterward as the United States Pottery Company, was established at Bennington, Vermont. Here, for a brief ten years, wares of such fine quality were produced that those of other excellent contemporary potteries are often overlooked by ceramic enthusiasts today. The man responsible for this was Christopher Webber Fenton. He came from a family of Connecticut potters who had moved to Bennington where there was already a pottery. This had been founded in 1793 by John Norton, producing kitchen earthenware through several generations until 1894.

Fenton married Louisa, granddaughter of John Norton, in 1832 and later entered into an uneasy partnership with his brother-in-law, Julius Norton. Fenton had no great skill as a potter. He was a promoter, with the virtues and failings of one. He had vision, knew how to acquire good potters, and invented a refinement of Rockingham ware known as "Patent Flint Enamel." This differed from the usual type in the manner of applying metallic colors. Previously they had been applied with a rag or brush. With Fenton's process the colors were finely ground and then dusted on, before firing, with an ordinary pepper shaker. The result was a brilliant tortoise-shell effect against a brown background. He patented the process, but potteries in other areas copied it so expertly that, unless a piece is marked, it is hard to tell its origin.

The partnership with Julius Norton was dissolved in 1847. Norton stayed with the family business and Fenton started the venture which made the name of Bennington famous. The variety of wares turned out in the decade from 1848 to 1858 was amazing in quantity. Among them were animal figures made in Rockingham flint enamel. Several former Staffordshire potters worked in Bennington, among them Daniel Greatback who had come to America to work for the Jersey City Pottery Company in 1840. He designed some of the finest Bennington pieces.

The reclining-doe flower-holder is one of them (Illustration 40). A companion to it is a stag with the same pose, coloring, and detail of base and flower-holder. Evidently this particular deer design was made only at Bennington. Both pieces bear the oval pottery mark of "Lyman Fenton & Co., Bennington, Vt.," and the date, 1849. Greatback was also well known for his lions, poodles, houndhandled pitchers, and cow creamers, several of which were adapted from English originals.

The stag was among the most favored of animal subjects in Europe and England from the eighteenth century on. Around 1765, Ralph Wood the elder, made a reclining stag with flower-holder in the form of a broken tree trunk. It had a soft lead glaze and the color harmony for which the potters of this famous family were noted.

### Salt Glaze, a Product of Staffordshire

The potteries of north Staffordshire, England, so famous for their fine earthenware from the middle of the eighteenth century, had begun in a modest way. Composed at first of small land-holding folk potters, what they made and their manner of working was similar to that practiced until a very short time ago in the southern mountains of America.

The difference between the two was that time moved on with the Staffordshire potters. Before the end of the seventeenth century, these craftsmen had advanced from butter crocks and other kitchenware items to the beginnings of fine earthenware for which they were later to attain world-wide reputation.

The first real change in method came when two brothers from the Continent started a pottery near the town of Burslem in 1693. They made tea and coffee pots and mugs in a black unglazed stoneware with raised and incised decorations which were forerunners of the basalt made famous by Josiah Wedgwood. These two potters, John and David Elers, would have preferred to keep their working ways secret but they needed two helpers. The two men they hired were ambitious local potters who stayed with them until they had learned their secrets. Then each started his own pottery in Shelton. For one of them, Thomas Astbury, the Elers' processes were just a beginning. He improved the technique of getting an exceedingly hard and transparent glaze by sprinkling quantities of common salt into his kilns while they were at high heat.

Known as salt glaze, ware so treated became one of the major products of Staffordshire and continued in favor until nearly the close of the eighteenth century when the newer queen's ware edged it out. One of the most important producers of salt glaze was Dr. Thomas Wedgwood II, a cousin of the great Josiah.

The ware during the early years was all white with decoration achieved by combining an incised geometric design with raised scrolls (Illustration 41). Later pieces omitted the embossed and incised motifs and substituted designs painted in enamel colors. There was naturally more variety with this latter method and floral patterns, country scenes, portraits of royalty and other prominent figures were used to good effect.

Meanwhile, from striving to imitate the weight and texture of Oriental porcelain, the copying of Chinese decorations naturally followed. The soup plate in Illustration 42 is an example of an early and quite successful attempt. The decorator had never been to the Orient nor had he ever had a chance to see a Chinese painter at work, but he could copy a pattern seen on a plate or other object from that far-off country.

This particular plate was made about 1750. It is decorated in the cobalt blue that was and still is a perennial favorite. It is hand-done in overglaze enamel colors. The central decoration is a faithful copy of the Chinese. The floral sprig border on the scalloped rim has more of an occidental flavor. The body is clear white with the transparent salt glaze slightly pock-marked.

All this was of course the forerunner of the much less expensive and colorful transfer-decorated earthenware which poured into the United States from shortly after the end of the War of 1812. During the heyday of salt glaze, which was roughly between 1725 and 1780, the Staffordshire area was a gloomy place on the days when salt was thrown into the kilns. Smoke of such density poured forth that it was twilight over the whole area for hours.

Other makers of this ware besides Thomas Astbury and Dr. Wedgwood were Thomas and John Wedgwood, Thomas Heath, Aaron Wood, Ralph Daniel and John Badderly. Items made included tableware, tea and coffee services, punch bowls, vases, figurines, and figure groups. Among the latter were the well-known pew groups, showing a courting couple, ill at ease in their best clothes, self-consciously holding hands.

41

## Whieldon's Tortoise-Shell Ware

Among the Staffordshire wares that preceded the popular blue and white transfer dishes of the early nineteenth century, was a multi-colored one known as tortoise-shell. Its originator was Thomas Whieldon, a contemporary of Josiah Wedgwood and next in importance to that great potter.

Whieldon achieved this tortoise-shell effect by using a cream-colored body as the base over which blurred patches of color were dusted. These were chiefly browns, ranging from very dark to straw-color, with greens and blues sometimes added for variety. Over all was a transparent lead glaze which gave a delicate sheen to the ware.

Pieces made were teapots (Illustration 43), coffee pots, cream pitchers, sugar bowls, salt dishes, cups and saucers, bowls, mugs, dessert services and decorative bowls. This ware became nearly, if not quite, as popular as his "collyflower," perfected just a little earlier. American colonists were buying it by 1760, and it was standard stock with importers until the American Revolution temporarily checked shipments of British goods.

In Staffordshire, other potters copied Whieldon's tortoise-shell, just as they did his cauliflower ware, and included it in their standard products. There seems to have been no hard feelings about this borrowing of another man's invention. Like a recipe in cooking, the results varied at the hands of less skilled or less experienced potters. With the exception of Wedgwood, Whieldon made the best tortoise-shell dishes and the competition of his fellow potters did not worry him. As for Josiah Wedgwood, he and Whieldon were partners at the time cauliflower and tortoise wares were originated. Consequently, the tortoise-shell dishes made at their two potteries after the brief partnership ended were superior to all others.

Among dishes shipped to America, teapots, sugar bowls and creamers were apparently more numerous than other pieces, since they are not too scarce today. Whieldon never marked his wares, so far as is known, but his tortoise-shell can be recognized by the clearance and sparkle of the glaze. Wedgwood made less of this ware, being more interested in perfecting and producing his queen's ware, and consistently marked his pieces except for some early ones.

Whieldon's teapots were usually small, like others of that century when tea was a very costly item. Almost spherical in shape, they had raised scroll decorations on handles and spouts. There was also a design of either raised flower and foliage or of a Chinese human figure. A small rosette of conventionalized leaves generally made the handle of the lid. The raised decoration was accomplished by using molds with incised designs.

Tortoise-shell should not be confused with agate-ware. The latter was made of clays of several colors, including some stained blue by adding cobalt, which were thoroughly kneaded until a resemblance to natural agate was attained.

During the time that Whieldon and Wedgwood were partners (1754-1759), there was an agreement that each man should carry on his experiments separately and not be obliged to exchange information. The two men must, however, have pooled their knowledge in the development of one ware. That was the "collyflower," as it was popularly called in its day. Whieldon had taken the ordinary white bisque, experimented with colors in lead glaze, modeled dishes in the forms of fruits and vegetables, and so produced excellent likenesses of melons, pineapples, and cabbages. Wedgwood perfected the color tone and, between them, a new ware was launched to compete with the popular blue and white.

Called "collyflower" ware, though no actual representation of that vegetable ever appeared, it took its name from the color of the leaf, a deep green. Pieces made included such hollow forms as teapots, coffee pots, milk pitchers, sugar bowls, and mugs, as well as salt dishes, mustard pots, and leaf-shaped plates. For covered dishes, the melon shape was probably the favorite (Illustration 44). This example has the clear yellow of the fruit; the plate beneath is leaf-shaped and in the green from which the ware takes its name. It was made by Wedgwood, about 1770. Advertisements in New York, Philadelphia, and Boston papers, between 1760 and 1775, telling of china "just imported" from England, made frequent references to "collyflower" ware and indicate that it had an appreciative public in the colonies as well as in England.

### Josiah Wedgwood and His Jasperware

Of all Staffordshire potters, probably none did so much to advance the craft, both artistically and commercially, as Josiah Wedgwood. Born in Burslem in 1730, he started his career at the age of fourteen as a potter's apprentice. Before he was thirty he had his own business and had begun his unceasing experiments for producing newer and better wares.

He showed signs from the beginning of being both a master potter and a good business man. He had a talent for knowing what the public wanted and also believed and practiced the belief that superior quality paid dividends. He would not tolerate imperfect pieces and on more than one occasion was known to have broken an offending ceramic object with his cane, rather than have it sold to the detriment of the Wedgwood reputation.

Only a few years after his first pottery was established in Burslem, he bought a tract of 150 acres and began building his Etruria factory. This name is still impressed on Wedgwood pieces, with Barleston, the works built some fifteen years ago, now added. His cream-colored queen's ware was the backbone of his business, but he was constantly experimenting with other wares. During the 1760's, he established a shop and warehouse in London, opened a Liverpool branch with an eye to the American trade, and brought out a descriptive catalogue of his wares which was printed in several languages. He also found time for such civic matters as better roads through the Staffordshire area and other improvements in transportation, so that the products of the various Staffordshire potteries might be shipped to the outside world easily and cheaply.

The invention of jasperware was Wedgwood's master accomplishment. To the amateur, this beautiful ceramic and the Wedgwood name have long been synonymous. He began his experiments with it in 1773 and perfected it four years later. A hard, unglazed stoneware, it took its name from its resemblance to the semi-precious stone, jasper, both in texture and color. This

43

was obtained by adding carbonate and sulphate of barium to a semi-porcelain clay and then using a metal oxide for the desired color. Blue is the most familiar, but there are six others—pale green, greyish green, pink, lilac, yellow, and black. Against this colored background, a raised white decoration produced a cameo effect.

Articles made in this ware were mainly display pieces—vases, covered cups, urns, pitchers, and bowls. Tea sets, plates (Illustration 45), and other items were made, but were probably more for display than for use. Wedgwood had the good sense to employ artists and craftsmen of high quality, such as James Tassie, John Flaxman, and William Hackwood. These men modeled the originals in wax for many of the jasperware pieces, including the portrait medallions that were set in some of the fine mantels and furniture of the Hepplewhite years.

William Hackwood, who modeled the Dance of the Hours vase (Illustration 46a), was Wedgwood's right-hand man in the modeling shop. He began working there in 1769 and was still in charge of modeling jasperware and basalt decorations for some thirty-seven years after the great Josiah's death in 1795. His portrait busts and medallions show that he could have been a sculptor of reputation. Well-known examples include portrait reliefs of George III, David Garrick, and Wedgwood himself.

Designs on the Hackwood vase and the accompanying wine pitcher by John Flaxman (Illustration 46b) reflect Wedgwood's partiality for classic art which was in high favor during his years as master potter. Vases and urns portraying classic figures in various poses were produced in fair numbers between 1780 and 1790, the height of the Adam influence in architecture, furniture, and decorative accessories. Flaxman, who modeled the original design of this wine pitcher, began work for Wedgwood in 1775 when only twenty years old. This particular pitcher was made both in jasperware and in black basalt. Flaxman models were used interchangeably in both wares but jasperware remained the favorite.

As with all ceramic innovations, other potters tried their hands at jasperware but with indifferent results. Two exceptions were friendly rivals of Wedgwood. John Turner was fairly successful but the body color of his ware was inferior and his white raised decoration over-ornate. William Adams, who had served his apprenticeship under Wedgwood, produced jasperware so well done that the pottery marks are the chief means of telling an Adams piece from a Wedgwood. His mark is "W. Adams," either impressed or printed. Wedgwood pieces have the impressed circular mark of "WEDGWOOD AND BENTLEY" or simply, "WEDGWOOD" if done after 1781, the year Bentley, the London partner, died.

Today, small articles in jasperware, cameo-like medallions for brooches, rings, small boxes, seals, and other kinds of jewelry, are popular with collectors who often have them set in gold mountings.

### Old Copper Lustre

Of the three types of lustre-ware perfected by Staffordshire potters in the latter years of the eighteenth century, copper was the first and most widely

44

produced. Although a potter there named Hancock is credited with the rediscovery of this ancient Persian over-glaze, it was Josiah Spode who perfected it. Wedgwood, always at the forefront in the search for better decoration, soon achieved a gold lustre that varied in tone from pink to purple, and shortly afterward a silver lustre.

Copper lustre was not only the least expensive of the three but lent itself to a variety of decorative effects, ranging from solid copper color in stripes and bands to resist and relief designs against a pastel background. A good grade of white earthenware was ordinarily used for the body of pieces so decorated. An exception was the factory at New Hall where only porcelain was used.

The most intricate of the decorative treatments was the resist. The pattern was painted on the unglazed body with glycerin. Then the piece was coated with a metallic solution and set aside until partly dry when it was washed in clear water. The glycerin disappeared along with the metallic coating but that painted directly on the clay body resisted the water and remained. From this came the name as well as many beautiful and complicated patterns.

Floral designs against a background of light blue, buff, green, or other soft colors were very popular. Quite often these were painted in contrasting colors after the glaze had been fired. Transfer-printed designs were also used under a thin lustre to decorate the body of a piece, especially a pitcher.

Pastel bands with relief decoration show the influence of Wedgwood's jasperware motifs. The designs were many and varied, with floral patterns probably most in favor and animal figures a close second. Pastoral vignettes were also used. Objects in copper lustre included pitchers of varied sizes and shapes, goblets, vases, bowls, and complete tea sets (Illustration 47). These pieces, made between 1820 and 1835, are good examples of resist and relief decoration. The top row shows goblets at right and left with light blue bands and resist decoration in a floral pattern; the pitcher in the center also has a light blue band on the body with a hunting pattern in relief. In the center row, left to right, pitcher and bowl are relief-decorated against a blue background but the pitcher at the right has a floral resist pattern against a buff background. The bottom row shows cups and saucers, sugar bowl, and teapot of a tea set that originally had eighteen cups and saucers, teapot, hot-water pot, sugar bowl, and creamer. Here cream-colored bands ornamented with sprays of flowers and pastoral vignettes in relief contrast with the rich copper lustre.

Copper lustre in its varied forms of decoration was made in Staffordshire and other English potteries from about 1800 to 1860. Some of it is marked with either an impressed name or letter; much of it bears no mark. Most of the Staffordshire potters made this ware. Minton, Spode, Wedgwood, and a few others marked their pieces with their names. Plain or marked, a large amount reached the United States and, by the mid-nineteenth century, there were comparatively few homes without one piece at least of this richly colored ware, often a small or medium-size creamer.

Both pink and silver lustre-wares were also in demand by those who could afford them. The latter was first made in imitation of silverware. The pieces had the silver glaze inside and out, and were shaped and decorated in the silversmithing style of the period. This held for some of the copper pieces also.

45

Pink was mostly used for bands, stripes, scrolls, and designs done in silhouette against the white body of a piece.

Like copper, silver lent itself to resist decoration. Designs were many and intricate, with polychrome colors added. Lustre pitchers were produced in quantity since there was always a ready market for them and the opportunity for variety in shape and decorative detail was practically limitless.

Pitchers decorated with silver lustre are now considered the most desirable. Gold in its shadings from pink to purple ranks second. High in favor, too, are silver lustre tea sets. The one in Illustration 48 is an elaborate example of the resist lustre type and was made in Staffordshire about 1810. The shape of the pieces is late eighteenth-century. The decoration is a floral pattern in polychrome colors against a silver background.

### The Ralph Woods and Their Figurines

Ceramic likenesses of human beings, animals, and birds were produced in Staffordshire as early as 1725. Some of the finest ever made came from the kilns of the Ralph Woods, father and son. They were members of a potting family whose history went back to nearly the start of the craft there and continued to about the middle of the nineteenth century. Ralph the elder was born in 1715 and died in 1772. During his early years he made salt-glaze ware but about 1760 turned to the making of fine figurines.

Among the outstanding characteristics of their work are the colors which are delicate and clear under a translucent lead glaze. The modeling is especially fine and was probably done by John Voyez, a French sculptor who worked in the area for a number of years. The bodies of the figures, for example, are well-proportioned and posed as a sculptor would arrange such subjects.

This is apparent in the figure of Sir Isaac Newton (Illustration 49). The pose is clearly that of the scientist lecturing before some distinguished group such as the Royal Society. His left hand grasps a telescope and with his right he lifts a drapery to reveal a globe. His court dress shows the delicate colors for which the Wood figures are famous. Made about 1790, the piece is inscribed "Ra. Wood, Burslem" on the back of the base in incised letters.

Among the best known figures by Ralph Wood I, the companion pieces, "Farmer and Wife," and "Old Age" (Illustration 50) are notable for coloring, pose, and lifelike quality. His bird figures also were usually done in pairs. One of his largest figures, "Reclining Stag," measures thirteen inches high by nine and one-half inches wide in contrast to the companion pieces, already mentioned, which are only eight and one-half inches high.

His son Ralph (1748-1795) worked with him and continued producing figurines after his father's death. Both men marked a considerable number of their figures and, in fact, were the first to impress their names on such objects. Ralph Wood II also numbered his pieces. In addition to the statuette of Sir Isaac Newton, he modeled a portrait bust of George Washington, a Madonna and Child, "Haymaker and Companion," and the well-known "Vicar and Moses" (Illustration 51). This last was made about 1780 and was so popular that it was copied by other potters for some fifty years afterward. Early examples have the mark "Ra. Wood." Copies are unmarked. Classed as a group figure, it shows the vicar in wig and clericals sleeping in his pulpit, leaving his sermon to be read by his clerk, Moses, who stands in a smaller enclosure immediately beneath.

The best of the Ralph Wood figures were done before 1780. Ralph Wood I died in 1772. After that date, over-glaze enamels were substituted for the earlier and more artistic under-glaze colors for which the finest of these figures were noted.

Enoch Wood, a cousin of Ralph, worked from 1780 until his death in 1846. His training included that of modeler and his most famous piece was done only a year after he had established his own pottery. It was a bust of the eminent divine, John Wesley. Enoch did it from life while the father of Methodism was his house guest. It proved such a popular figure that Wood continued to produce it in both pottery and black basalt for nearly sixty years. America was one of his best markets and for it he did various figures, particularly statuettes of Washington and Franklin. During his latter years he made and sent to America rustic figurines, sometimes in pairs as candlesticks, and early Victorian sentimental subjects.

### Caricatures in Pottery

The name "Toby" seems to have been early associated with conviviality. There was Sir Toby Belch in Shakespeare's *Twelfth Night* who was fat, boisterous, given to hard drinking and staying out nights; there was Toby Shandy in Laurence Sterne's *Tristam Shandy*, published in 1760; and the next year appeared an English print with verses describing—

> "Old Toby Philpot, as thirsty a soul
> As e'er drank a bottle or fathomed a bowl."

It is believed that John Voyez, the sculptor, who worked in Staffordshire for many years, modeled the early type of toby jug from this print. These jugs were a noted creation of Ralph Wood. Toby jugs in a variety of forms were popular from the 1760's until late in the nineteenth century and were widely made by various English potteries as well as by a few in America. The typical toby is a comic depiction of a short fat fellow, comfortably seated, with a jug on his knee and wearing a three-cornered hat (Illustration 52). Sometimes he has a pipe as well as a jug, and sometimes his faithful dog is crouched at his feet.

Most of the Ralph Wood tobies were of this sort, but he also produced his "Thin Man," "Gin Woman," "King Hal," and the "Hearty Good Fellow," the latter a smiling urbane figure with jug and pipe. Ralph's cousin, Enoch Wood, also made toby jugs, such as "Night Watchman," and a standing representation of Benjamin Franklin taking a pinch of snuff.

Other Staffordshire potters who made these jugs included Whieldon, John Davenport, David Wilson, Lakin and Poole, Palmer and Neale, and Pratt of Fenton. Nor were all the tobies masculine. In addition to Ralph Wood's "Gin Woman," there was the famous "Martha Gunn," made by Davenport about 1820, which took its name from the nursemaid of the infant Prince of Wales. A female toby was also made in Rockingham brown. Another, known as "Toby's Wife," represented a seated woman wearing a tall mob-cap.

47

As time went on the subjects varied widely from the original. In addition to genre and allegorical figures, there were such historical ones as Nelson, Napoleon, Wellington, Howe, and the Duke of York. There were also several versions of John Bull. Sometimes he was shown with one arm akimbo for a handle and the other uplifted to form a spout; sometimes he sat stiffly with one hand on his knee, the other hanging loosely at his side. The name of the subject sometimes appears on the base; sometimes there is a date, but not often is the maker's mark present.

The most colorful tobies were made in Staffordshire, but excellent ones were produced at Rockingham in the characteristic brown. American-made tobies were also of this type and were turned out at Bennington and similar potteries.

The usual size for antique toby jugs is about ten inches in height, though smaller ones and even condiment pots, made in Staffordshire until well into the nineteenth century, are to be found. Demand by collectors for these amusing old jugs began early in the twentieth century and many reproductions have resulted. Among them, tobies of blue and white Delft were made in Holland in the early 1920's. There are also present-day tobies of such prominent personalities as Winston Churchill, Franklin D. Roosevelt, General MacArthur, and Field Marshal Viscount Montgomery.

### The Romantic Figures of Chelsea

Little porcelain statuettes and similar ornamental figures came into favor in Europe quite early in the eighteenth century, the fashion having been brought from China by way of the trade routes. Those of Meissen appeared first.

By 1745, the vogue for such mantel and cabinet ornaments had become so widespread in England that the time was ripe for their domestic manufacture. Accordingly, two porcelain factories, Bow and Chelsea, were established before the first half of the century was over. Ten years later, a third, was founded at Derby and eventually absorbed the first two.

The story of the Chelsea figures involves the Flemish artist, Nicholas Sprimont, who was director of the works from 1750 to 1769, and the French sculptor, Louis Roubiliac, who was associated with the factory during much of that time. Sprimont, an artist and silversmith of ability, was also a good businessman and the venture grew. Like so many of the porcelain manufacturers of the period, Sprimont had a rich patron who aided the company at the outset. This was the Duke of Cumberland and, according to old records, he underwrote the expenses by making a yearly grant. The factory also had the royal patronage of both George II and George III. The latter, who came to the throne in 1760, gave several large orders that called for the work of skilled artists.

Sprimont gave the public what it wanted and produced about everything that could be made of porcelain. Soon he had a warehouse in London for the sale of his products where, in addition to regular business, annual auctions of two of more weeks duration took place. For close to twenty years, the products of Chelsea were in high favor, particularly the statuettes and figurines.

Sprimont was fortunate in having the artistic skill and ability of Roubiliac,

48

*(Illustration 50)* "Old Age," by Ralph Wood I, ca. 1765.

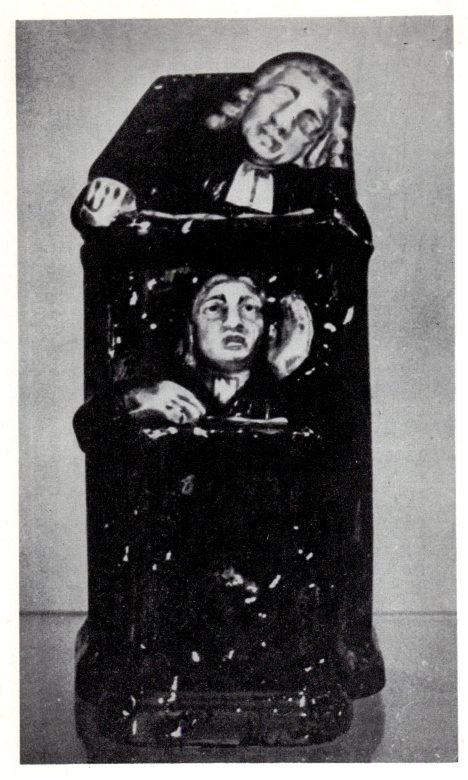

*(Illustration 51)* "The Vicar and Moses," by Ralph Wood II.

*(Illustration 52)* **A Toby Jug, by Ralph Wood I, ca. 1765.**

(*Illustration 53*) A Pair of Romantic Chelsea Porcelain Figures, ca. 1765.

(*Illustration 54*) Worcester Porcelain Plates and Compote, ca. 1810. Plate at left and matching compote have reserves done in flower, fruit, and bird motifs. Plate at right is an Imari pattern.

(Illustration 55) A Derby Dessert Service, ca. 1790.

(Illustration 56) Bone China Teapot and Tray, by Spode, ca. 1810-1820.

*(Illustration 57)* Bone China Dessert Service with Painted Bird Decoration by Spode, ca. 1815.

*(Illustration 58)* English Bone China with Gilt Decoration, ca. 1830-1850.

(Illustration 59) An Assortment of Wedding-Band China. The plates with fluted or plain rims are unmarked English bone china, 1830-1870, and the bowl is attributed to the Tucker factory of Philadelphia.

*(Illustration 60)* Above, English Ironstone Covered Dish and Platter, ca. 1850.
*(Illustration 61)* Below, Pair of Victorian Staffordshire Spaniels, ca. 1850.

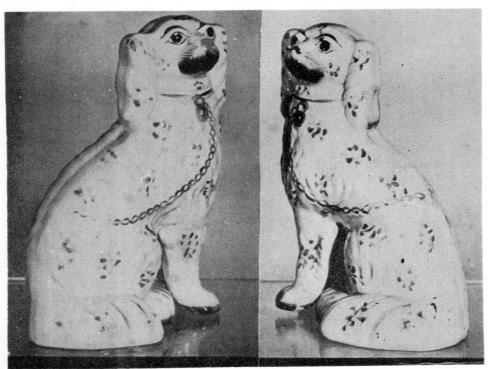

*(Illustration 62)* Staffordshire Chicks-in-Nest Covered Dish, ca. 1860.

(Illustration 63) Nineteenth-Century Dresden Porcelain Figures.

*(Illustration 64)* German and Austrian Porcelain Figures, ca. 1750-1780. Left to right these are: a gallant playing flute, from Ludwigsburg; youth holding floral chain, Vienna; trinket peddler, Hochst; and nymph, also Ludwigsburg.

*(Illustration 65)* **Old Paris Plates and Sauce Tureen, ca. 1845.**

*(Illustration 66)* Delft Plate, with Decoration in Blue Copied from the Chinese, ca. 1750.

*(Illustration 67a)* **Oriental Lowestoft Teapot with Arms of New York Decoration, ca. 1800.**

*(Illustration 67b)* **Oriental Lowestoft Tureen with Fitzhugh-type Decoration in Blue, ca. 1825.**

who had studied under a Saxon modeler in Paris, to assist him. Naturally not all of the figures made at Chelsea can be attributed to him, especially since he died in 1762, but his influence and ideas contributed much to the beauty of such romantic pieces as are shown in Illustration 53. Typical of the glamorized rustics which were so often the subjects of Chelsea figures, the one at the left is of a young man seated on a tree stump playing a bagpipe with his dog beside him, the whole surrounded by a floral background. The young woman at the right is playing a mandolin and has a lamb at her side. Both figures have rococo bases.

Sprimont's health began to fail in the late 1750's, and in 1769 he sold his factory, retired with a comfortable fortune but died within a year. The Chelsea works were then absorbed by the factory at Derby. Chelsea figures during the Sprimont years were the finest in England. They were popular in America also, as were other products of this factory. The first gift that Benjamin Franklin sent home to his wife in Philadelphia, after he went to London as colonial agent in the 1760's, was a Chelsea tea service with a sprigged pattern. The teapot is still in existence.

Not all Chelsea porcelains were marked. When used, the mark during the Sprimont era was a small anchor in an oval medallion.

### Worcester and Its Porcelains

The first china factory in Worcester, England, was started in the mid-eighteenth century when fifteen citizens organized the Worcester Tonkin Manufacture and subscribed forty-five hundred pounds for the venture.

A physician, Dr. John Wall, who had first conceived the project, was their leader while among his fellow-founders were an apothecary, an engraver, a silversmith, and two experienced potters. Business plans were carefully made and speedily carried out. An old mansion was leased in July of 1751 as a factory, kilns were built, and a staff of workmen engaged.

Dr. Wall had business aptitude and the porcelain factory was successful from the start. These early years are known as the Dr. Wall period and the products are among the most beautiful of English china. Dr. Wall apparently had some of the best artists then working in England at china painting. At first, the factory made only tableware, copying the pieces imported from China as to shape and decoration. Later decorations included transfer prints from copperplate engravings and, around 1768, came the exotic bird patterns that are almost synonymous with the name Worcester.

After Dr. Wall's death, the business was bought in 1783 by Thomas Flight, agent of the company at its London warehouse. He put his two sons, Joseph and John, in charge of the factory. They introduced more ornate decorations, changing the character of the ware. Consequently, porcelains of the Flight period are not hard to distinguish from the earlier Wall examples. Furthermore, Robert Chamberlain, head of the decorating department, decided to open his own porcelain factory, taking his brother Humphrey with him. This did not make for particularly good feeling, but both factories prospered and were keen rivals.

In 1793 the Flights took in Martin Barr as a partner and, fourteen years later, Martin Barr the younger joined them. Name and mark were then changed

49

to Barr, Flight & Barr. The three pieces in Illustration 54 were made early in this period which lasted to 1840 when the rival companies merged and became Chamberlain & Company. Lastly, in 1862, the name was changed to its present one, Worcester Royal Porcelain Company, Ltd., a joint-stock company still operating.

Marks used from the founding of the original company to 1840 were first, a W in script, then a more usual mark, a crescent in outline, in solid color, or with shaded lines. These, as well as the marks "R. H. Worcester" or "R. Hancock, fecit" belong to the Dr. Wall period. China bearing any one of these marks is the rarest and most artistic. Marks after 1783 include names or initials of the firm, impressed.

Although china made during the Barr, Flight, & Barr years tended to be over-ornate, the quality was excellent and many handsome dinner services were produced, along with tea sets, dessert services, and other objects. The Chinese influence persisted from the start. The Imari pattern, shown on the plate at the right in the illustration, was later adapted by Staffordshire potters to produce the Gaudy Dutch dishes with the vivid colors which give it its present-day name.

### Old Derby Porcelain

The English factory which produced the china now known as Crown Derby was started in the town of that name in 1755 by William Duesbury, a young ceramic modeler and enameller. He had previously worked in London, then at Longton Hall in Staffordshire, and finally settled in the town which his porcelain factory was to make famous.

His chief products at first were figures, so popular at the time and easily sold. As he prospered he acquired other porcelain factories noted for their fine products. He bought the first one, Chelsea, in 1769 and operated it there for fifteen years, then transferred plant and workers to Derby. In 1776, the Bow works was bought and moved with a number of the workmen to Derby.

By this time he had a London warehouse and issued catalogues listing his porcelains, both ornamental and useful. The latter included table and dessert services. On the founder's death in 1786, his son, William, Jr., continued the business. The dessert service shown in Illustration 55 was made during the years he headed the company. It is typical of the designs popular at Derby. These, unlike some of the other porcelain factories of the time, showed little foreign influence but were distinctly English, in fact, reflected the silversmithing styles of the period. The compote in the center of the bottom row is a striking example. It and the other pieces are part of a service for twenty. The top row shows a pair of oval sauce tureens with stands and a plate. The bottom row a pair of valanced oval dishes flanking the compote. The painted decoration is in iron red, blue, purple, and gilt with borders of scrolling, foliage, and pendent urn motifs.

The pottery mark used during this Duesbury II period, 1786-1794, is a crown surrounded by "Duesbury Derby" in gold with crossed batons added. A third William Duesbury inherited the factory in 1796. He sold it in 1809 to his manager, Robert Bloor. On the latter's death, it passed to two other workmen who failed to make it profitable. Finally it was sold to a Staffordshire firm and the works were closed in 1848.

Some of the Bloor craftsmen were later engaged by Sampson Hancock for work in a small factory at Derby where former styles were reproduced. In 1876 the Derby Crown Porcelain Company, Ltd., was formed and in 1890 became the Royal Crown Derby Porcelain Company. Under this name it has continued to the present day and so qualifies as one of the longest-lived porcelain works in England.

### English Bone China

Bone china takes its name from the fact that finely powdered cattle bones are added to the mixture of clay and ground china stone. It was the successful English substitute for the kaolin porcelain of China. A century before, these Chinese dishes had come into favor with Europeans but, because of the long hazardous voyage, they were very expensive.

By 1750 various English potteries were trying to devise a substitute. The Bow pottery in Essex, that of Chelsea, close to London, Derby, Worcester, and Bristol, all tried unsuccessfully to create a satisfactory ware that could be made economically enough for the popular market.

It was finally accomplished about 1800 by Josiah Spode II. He had succeeded his father, Josiah I, known as "Old" Spode, in 1797. The elder Spode, who had earlier worked for Josiah Wedgwood, established his pottery in 1770. He was particularly successful in making the cobalt blue dishes of earthenware, long a chief product of the Staffordshire area. At the same time he started experiments with bone ash in the search for a substitute for the Chinese porcelain clay. His son continued this and perfected it, using china clay and feldspar mixed with bone ash in nearly equal proportions. It resulted in a substance halfway between the hard paste of China and the soft paste of eighteenth-century English porcelain factories. The durability of the one was present as well as the softer quality of the other. Its color was halfway between the bluish white of the Oriental and the creamy white of the soft paste. It was also less liable to chip than the hard-paste porcelain.

A practical and economical solution of the porcelain formula problem, bone china became standard with all English potteries and, with only minor changes in proportions, is still made in quantity. At the time Spode was perfecting this type of china, the factories at Worcester and Derby were the important producers, but it was not long before the bone china trade shifted to Staffordshire where Spode and his competitors, Minton, Davenport, and others, developed this new product.

The Spode pottery sold large quantities of this finer ware for export to the United States. Josiah II had as a partner William Copeland, originally his traveling salesman. Both men died within a year of each other—1826 and 1827. They were succeeded briefly by Josiah III who died in 1833. The next owner was William Taylor Copeland, an alderman of the City of London and later its Lord Mayor. He changed the pottery's mark from "Spode" to "Copeland" and then to "Copeland and Garrett, Late Spode." Finally the mark became a small oblong lettered "Spode" with "Copeland" above. This pottery is still in existence and very active.

During the years when much of the china now considered antique was being made, from 1800 to 1860, marking was a casual matter, with the potter

51

deciding how much or how little of his wares should bear the impress of the firm. The Derby factory mark, for instance, was a crown above a capital D, but a good proportion of old Derby bears no mark. Minton, Spode, and Davenport were usually marked, although all the pieces of a large dinner service might not be. In Illustration 56, the teapot, a floral design in naturalistic colors, was made at the Spode pottery between 1810 and 1820 as part of a set, but bears no mark itself.

Josiah Spode II favored Chinese designs of exotic birds against a floral background, but did not neglect the English type of decoration. Among his most pleasing patterns are those of familiar English birds painted in their natural habitat, as in Illustration 57. This dessert service of twelve plates and a compote was made about 1815. The plate at the right shows a dove perched on a bough; that at the left, a lark against a slightly different background. These simple scenes are painted in naturalistic colors. An added decoration is a raised floral pattern in white on plate and compote borders. Here each piece bears the name "Spode" impressed.

Illustration 58 shows bone china with a Victorian flavor. It is gilt-decorated in banding and leaf patterns. From left to right they are: teacup and saucer, unmarked but dating between 1830 and 1850; cake plate, originally part of a tea service, decorated with leaf scrolls divided by tapering radiating bands, bearing the Derby mark, and dating from about 1840; unmarked chocolate cup and saucer, 1820 to 1835, with simple scroll pattern.

### Gilt Wedding-Band China

Although rarely mentioned or illustrated in reference books on old china, I consider the design popularly known as "wedding band" one of the most interesting of those produced during the early years of the Victorian period. Yet the price range for individual dishes or entire services is considerably more moderate than that for other porcelains of the same age.

My own collection started with an assortment of plates which came to me from the home of a Vermont great-uncle. I was impressed by the brilliant whiteness of the glaze, the effective modeling of their fluted rims and the uniform quality of the overglaze gold banding. Also, the bottoms of the plates have the ringed bases raised as much as three-sixteenths of an inch, a characteristic of the more carefully made and earlier examples of mid-nineteenth-century china.

With these inherited dishes as a beginning, I started to assemble a dinner service. Buying pieces here and there over a period of six or eight years, I gathered some pertinent facts about this kind of china from dealers and by studying examples which I saw and handled. Why it is called "wedding band" is not known, but the likeness between the banding and the wide wedding rings of the Victorian period makes the name apt and explains why it is now the accepted one.

Many of us born in the last decade of the nineteenth century can probably remember our grandparents' dining table set with a white porcelain chastely decorated with a wide gold band. Not new even then, since it had probably been among their wedding gifts, it was cherished and used for special occasions. We now regard it with nostalgic eyes as part of a leisurely, comfortable way of life, long since gone. But for those who arrived in the world several decades after the end of the Victorian era, these same dishes have an appealing quaintness. Hence, there is a growing demand for this design.

Wedding-band china was made by the porcelain factories of England and France from about 1830 to 1870 when it was superseded by the more colorful services with floral decorations. During its heyday, it was much in vogue as the best china of many American homes. That of English provenance is bone china and practically never bears a pottery mark, though much of it has underglaze production marks such as Arabic or Roman numerals or small devices, triangles and the like, to identify the work of individual workmen.

French wedding-band porcelain is quite often marked. It may have the initials C. F. H. in small size, hand-done with a fine brush in green or red, considered an early mark of Charles Haviland, who acquired a factory at Limoges in 1840. Another fairly common mark, usually in black, is the outline of a tall baluster-shaped vase with the initials B. D. above an L. I believe it to be the mark of another of the Limoges factories but have not yet been able to identify it. Other French marks include "Ed. Honoré à Paris," "Mft. de Lefebvre, Rue Amlot" and "K. et G. Lundville."

There is also the tradition that the Tucker pottery of Philadelphia produced china of this design, unmarked, but so closely resembling that of European provenance that there is no way of identifying the pieces. If any wedding-band china was made at this American factory, it would date from 1832 to 1838 when the venture was at the height of its commercial success.

As to age, wedding-band china with the fluted rim is earliest (Illustration 59). The unfluted dishes date from about 1850, as do the octagon-shaped covered dishes, platters, teapots, and the like.

### Ironstone China from Staffordshire

Ironstone china, the name of which well describes this hardy ware, was designed as an inexpensive substitute for the costly and fragile bone china. It was originated by Miles Mason who had been a china dealer in London. In 1780 he took over the Lane Delph pottery in Staffordshire and started making earthenware transfer-decorated dishes with designs in the Chinese manner known as "British Nankin."

These were popular and sold well, but Mason is best remembered for his ironstone china for which he and his son, Charles, obtained a patent in 1813. The body of this ware was of white clay with generous quantities of pulverized flint and slag from iron-smelting added. As a result it was very strong and not easily chipped. Though heavier than real porcelain, it was very popular in England and America for a half-century. As soon as the Mason patent expired or even before, most of the other Staffordshire potters were making china of about the same formula which they marked "ironstone" or some similar descriptive term.

Its originator marked his, "Mason's Patent Ironstone China," printed in black and surmounted by the outline of a crown. Decorations on his dishes ranged from highly colored and gilded all-over patterns to a simple strawberry design in copper lustre.

From about 1835 to 1860, octagon-shaped dishes were especially popular in table ware and much of the ironstone china was produced in that form by the various Staffordshire potters, including Wedgwood and Spode. The Mason family retired in 1851, selling their pottery to a corporation headed by a member of the Ridgway family. Ironstone china popular with Americans included transfer-decorated dishes in the Willow pattern, some American blue and white historic and scenic designs, usually done in deep blue, the copper-lustre strawberry pattern already mentioned, and undecorated, like the covered dish in Illustration 60. This dish bears the design registry mark of T. & R. Boote, a firm founded in 1842 by Thomas and Richard Boote in Burslem. The mark, a diamond-shape with circle above enclosing a Roman numeral IV, has numerals and letters by which the date of dish can be told. The potter's mark is impressed in a lozenge below. The platter in the illustration is unmarked and is of the shape so much in favor during the early Victorian years. The irregularly fluted edge, brushed with cobalt, was a popular decorative touch for plates and platters in this ware. Occasionally, a covered dish so decorated is found. This simple design was copied from an earlier Leeds pattern.

Most ironstone china bears the mark of its maker and, from 1842 on, a design registry may be present if the piece is of a special shape or pattern. When unmarked, weight and feel of a piece identify it.

### Staffordshire Dog Figures

English potters, particularly those of Staffordshire, were most versatile. In addition to a wide variety of useful wares, they also produced ornamental pieces of all kinds. Among their decorative objects, figures of dogs were favorites, probably because the English have always been an animal-loving people.

Dog figures in either porcelain or earthenware were made at most of the important potteries. Finer ones of porcelain were produced in somewhat restricted numbers and in small sizes at Bow, Chelsea, Derby, and Worcester. At Staffordshire, on the other hand, those of earthenware were turned out by the thousands. These figures included spotted coach dogs, greyhounds, poodles, and whippets, but it was in their representations of the floppy-eared spaniels that the Staffordshire potters excelled.

They made them in all sizes, from miniatures not over an inch high to practically life-size ones as much as thirty inches tall. They were usually modeled in a sitting position and often made in facing pairs (Illustration 61). Many had an all-over brown glaze without added decoration, but the majority were produced in white with faces, fur markings, collars, and leaders in colors and gilt. The most popular colors were brown, red, or a deep shade of purple known as *aubergine*. Touches of gold were often added.

Smaller spaniels were made solely as shelf or cabinet ornaments; larger ones sometimes had a practical use. When modeled with the dog sitting on an oblong base, the figure was designed to be used as a door stop. Since the base was always a little larger than the dog, it protected the glaze of the latter from being scratched or chipped in the course of its somewhat hazardous use. Large-sized ones without bases were intended as mantel ornaments or for the tops of tall pieces of furniture, such as a flat-topped secretary or bookcase.

During Early Victorian years — about 1830 to 1860 — spaniels were fashionable as lap dogs and most Staffordshire spaniels were produced during these years. They were always modeled in a somewhat artificial pose with the head turned at right angles to the body. There was also an almost human cast of countenance to the face. This accounts for much of their appeal and charm to collectors today.

At first glance, these Staffordshire spaniels may look alike, but closer study reveals many slight variations. A physician of my acquaintance is very proud of his collection of over fifty pairs, all different. He gathered them over a period of years and is still on the lookout for another pair unlike any in his possession now. His spaniels are from three inches tall to nearly fourteen inches.

Probably because they were made in such numbers, the spaniels were not marked. So it is impossible to identify them further than to say that they are Staffordshire, made sometime between 1800 and 1860. Those of finer modeling and color are usually the earlier examples.

### Ancestors of the Glass Hen Dish

Covered dishes modeled as hen's nests, either full of newly-hatched chicks (Illustration 62) or surmounted by a maternal fowl, have a much longer history than the Victorian period with which they are usually associated. Their origin dates back into the eighteenth century when they were made of much finer material than either the earthenware or pressed-glass examples of the Victorian years. At Chelsea, Bow, and Derby, a great variety of porcelain table services, individual covered dishes, and decorative figures were made in the form of wild fowl. Skillfully modeled and colored, they were listed as "partridge sets" in the London auction catalogues before 1770. The quantities of such sets sold show that they were much in demand at the time.

These dishes went out of fashion for more than a generation. When they returned to favor, about seventy years later, their manufacture had shifted to Staffordshire and the material used was now glazed earthenware. Instead of being modeled after wild fowl, they were now designed in the form of the domestic hen—an understandable change since they were destined to join the other cottage ornaments, popularly known as "chimney pieces," on the shelf above the fireplace.

The nest dish in Illustration 62 is of this kind and dates from between 1840 and 1850. The three newly-hatched chicks are brown with white beaks and bead-like eyes. The broken shells are cream white. The poses, even of the one just emerging from its shell, are so realistic as to suggest that the artist modeled it from life. The basket nest is straw-brown with slight touches of green. Pleasing as was the anecdotal character of these covered dishes, they were not made in large quantity. Today, they are much rarer than other Staffordshire cottage ornaments.

Whether they were a specialty of only one or two potteries in the area or more widely made, cannot be established. The limited number that have survived bear no mark of a specific pottery as far as I can find out. Yet they were obviously produced from carefully modeled molds and expertly colored in a naturalistic style.

The last phase of this type of dish took place in the United States where several Middle Western glass factories produced covered hen dishes in quantity from about 1870 on. This is discussed in the Glass Section of this book.

## Meissen and Dresden

Back in the mid-nineteenth century, Dresden porcelains presented no problem of provenance to our forebears. It seemed perfectly clear to them that a small statue of a Dresden shepherdess or a romantic group for sale in an American china shop must have been imported from the city of Dresden in Saxony. Few were aware that these little figures had a Chinese ancestry, similar ornamental objects having come from the Orient by way of the trade routes, and that those they were looking at were actually made in a town a few miles from Dresden, named Meissen.

There is now considerable confusion as to which pieces should be classed as Meissen and which as Dresden, especially as they all come from the same factory. A hard-paste porcelain, similar to that produced in China, was invented in Dresden in 1709, and shortly afterwards a factory was established in Meissen for making articles of this fine substitute for the Oriental ware. This factory prospered to such a degree that for nearly a century it set the fashions for Continental and English porcelains. During all this time, the wares made at Meissen were known as Dresden china because that city was their chief market.

About twenty-five years ago, museum ceramic experts began calling this porcelain made before 1850, "Meissen," and the ware made after that date, "Dresden," and this classification generally holds true today. For example, in Illustration 63, the mythological group at the left dates from about 1830 and is therefore labelled "Meissen." It is a copy of an eighteenth-century piece by Kandler, one of the factory's greatest artists. The figures include a winged Eros in an orange mantle, Psyche in turquoise blue robes and, above them, Juno seated on a cloud and holding a floral garland. The goddess is attended by her familiar bird, a peacock.

The group at the right, dating from about thirty years later, is considered a Dresden piece and is Victorian in feeling. Two youthful lovers in bright costumes stand side by side before a white porcelain bust. At their feet are a dog and a lamb, and behind them an impish boy spying on them. These Dresden pieces continued to be made until after 1870 and can usually be identified by their colors, the excessive frilliness of costume, and the "smear-painted" hair on the heads of the figures, in contrast to the finer execution of the earlier Meissen figures.

### Derivatives of Meissen

A little over a hundred miles south of Berlin is the city of Dresden on the Elbe River in Saxony. Fourteen miles west and also in the Elbe Valley is the town of Meissen. Both these cities owe their fame as porcelain centers to a discovery made in Dresden which proved of great economic and social significance to the western world.

There, in 1709, Johann Friedrich Bottger, a young alchemist under the patronage of Augustus II, invented a hard-paste porcelain comparable to that produced in China. Shortly afterwards, a factory was established in a fortress in Meissen which thrived, and by 1730 had set the standard for all the great Continental and English porcelain houses.

The Meissen factory did not long have a monopoly either of its formula or of the wares that resulted. As early as 1718 the secret of this hard-paste porcelain had escaped to Vienna by way of two runaway employees, Stolzel and Hunger. These two, one a chemist and the other an enameler, helped Claude du Pacquier, a Hollander, to found a factory in the Austrian capital. After a checkered financial history, it was bought by the Empress Marie Theresa and became a royal enterprise in 1744.

More desertions of Meissen workmen occurred, resulting in other porcelain factories being erected in Germany and elsewhere. One of the chief peddlers of the Meissen porcelain technique was Joseph Jacob Ringler who left the Vienna factory in 1748. Directly or indirectly, he was responsible for ten new German ventures. Six of them prospered considerably, among them being Hochst (1746-1796) and Ludwigsburg (1788-1824).

These various factories all imitated the porcelains being made at Meissen which, however, still maintained its leadership until the Seven Years War when the Prussians looted the town and carried away thirty boxes of porcelains. Meissen workmen were marched off to Berlin to work in a factory that had already been started in 1750 by runaway workmen from Hochst.

While all of these factories made figures similar to Meissen, some paralleled it in quality of paste, others in glaze and decoration. The designs, however, tended to be too ornate. The figures in Illustration 64 are attributed to Vienna, Ludwigsburg, and Hochst. Figures at the extreme right and left were done at Ludwigsburg between 1750 and 1770. The Bacchic nymph sacrificing a goat is exceptionally well modeled, as is the eighteenth-century youth. The latter is claid in pale yellow breeches and is playing a flute. His dog at his feet is done in a most appealing pose. The genre figure of a peddler in blue breeches with a tray of bottles was made at Hochst in the late eighteenth century. Finally, there is the overly pretty figure of a youth in a figured yellow coat holding a floral chain. A typical example of the work done at Vienna around 1770, it is finely modeled but rather too ornate, like so much of the Vienna porcelain.

### Vieux Paris Porcelain

Among the potters of a century and more ago who often neglected to mark their wares, there were some thirty small porcelain factories and decorating shops in Paris that flourished from the closing years of the Napoleonic era to the Franco-Prussian War. These potters ornamented their wares in the French manner with a liberal use of gilt and colored enamel. There was no attempt to cater to American tastes as there was in the case of that produced at Limoges by Charles Haviland. Consequently, this Vieux Paris porcelain is not as well known in America as Limoges.

The Vieux Paris factories specialized in dinner and dessert services, and in large classic mantel urns and vases. The favorite types of ornamentation are clusters of fruits and flowers painted in full color (Illustration 65), architectural vignettes and small landscapes in either colors or in black and white, and genre groups in pastoral settings. These central decorations, or "reserves," are usually surrounded by wide bands of pink, known as *rose Pompadour,* cobalt blue, called *bleu du roi,* cornflower blue, apple green, buff, or ruby red, enhanced with gilt edging on the rim and inner side. The large two-handled mantel urns and vases are often entirely gilt or with a gilt ground framing painted panels of architectural subjects, landscapes, or floral medallions.

The quality of Vieux Paris is consistently fine. Many of the men who made it had worked earlier as decorators or potters at the Sèvres factory, beginning as apprentices and continuing until they went into business for themselves, either as porcelain makers or as decorators in the shops to which the former shipped their plain white wares for the painted decorations to be added.

The colored ornamentation and the banding and gilding was hand-painted; the decoration in black was sometimes transfer-printed. This latter method was brought to Paris in the late eighteenth century by an Englishman, appropriately named Charles Potter. However, the French craftsmen were more inclined to remain faithful to hand-painted methods. Vieux Paris, whether hand-painted or transfer-printed, is easily distinguished from English porcelain of the same period. The body is hard paste of a clear white translucence, and its evenness of glaze and the meticulousness of the hand-painting and gilding are readily apparent. The English porcelain of the period is of bone china, slightly creamy in tone, and there is much less use of gilt in its more restrained decoration. Generally, the shapes of the English and French porcelains are similar.

Although very little Vieux Paris porcelain is marked, occasionally pieces bear the maker's impress. "Mft. de Lefebure, Rue Amelot" and "Nast" are two of the marks commonly found. Vieux Paris porcelains can be considered worthwhile collectors' items, not only as antiques, but also for their inherent decorative qualities and fine craftsmanship.

### Blue and White Delft

When, some years before the 1890's, American collectors first became interested in antiques—"relics" to them—blue and white Delft plates, spinning wheels, and copper kettles were the fashionable things to collect. A small spinning wheel with its neatly turned legs and spokes provided antiquarian atmosphere in the living room or hall corner, while the décor of the dining room was dominated by Delft dishes on the wall or plate-rail, with a well-polished copper kettle added for contrast.

Today's collector leaves the spinning wheel for the museum room. The copper kettle, if present at all, goes where it belongs—near the fireplace. But blue and white Delftware still receives a place of honor in the corner cupboard or on the mantel shelf.

Delftware is not as plentiful as formerly, when there were dealers like the three Koopmans of Boston, New York, and Baltimore who were Delft specialists. Some of their pieces came from old families of Dutch descent but more of it was imported directly from the Netherlands. We can thank such dealers, who knew Delft well and were discriminating as to age and quality, for most of the pieces available today.

Delft takes its name from the town in Holland eight miles from the seaport of Rotterdam. Originally as famous for its beer as its porcelain, by 1650 Delft had become one of the important European pottery centers. Its specialty

58

was an earthenware coated with an opaque white, decorated with cobalt blue, and finished with a transparent lead glaze. For lightness, the clay used was a mixture of those brought from Tournai and Mulheim. The opaque white background resulted from a coating of tin oxide and an initial firing. Artists then did the painting in cobalt blue, often copying their designs from Chinese blue and white porcelains. A dusting with lead oxide for the transparent surface glaze and a second firing completed the making of a piece of blue and white Delft.

The variety of designs in the Chinese manner were inspired by Chinese dishes which ships of the Dutch East India Company brought to the seaports of the Low Countries. Hollanders, like many other Europeans, could not get enough of this costly Oriental porcelain. So the Delft potters obliged with their less expensive earthenware decorated in the Chinese manner. During the seventeenth century Delft had at least thirty-five master potters, each with his own pottery. There were as many more in the eighteenth century.

Examples of Delftware from about 1650 to 1725, when decoration was often the work of skilled artists, some of them painters of reputation, are museum rarities. Until about 1800 production of Delft for home use and export was increased. Artisan painters executed the decoration, usually in the Chinese manner. The plate in Illustration 66 is a good example. Made at Delft about 1750, it is about twelve inches across, has a cobalt blue decoration and opaque white background. The slender female figure in the center of the garden scene is of the "long Eliza" sort copied from Chinese porcelains of the late Ming period. The border of shaped panels interspersed by dotted diapering also approximates the Chinese.

In addition to plates, some of them fourteen to sixteen inches in diameter, the Delft potters also produced mugs, bowls, teapots, cow-shaped cream pitchers, vases, tobacco and apothecary jars, fireplace tiles, both Biblical and genre, and, occasionally, bird cages. The plates and jars are now the best known.

### Oriental China for the Western Trade

The story of Oriental Lowestoft involves patient Chinese potters in an inland city on the Yangtze River, hard-headed Cantonese merchants, avid western traders, sailing ships and well-appointed Occidental houses, some of them located on the New England coast and built with a "widow's walk."

European traders began knocking at the reluctant gates of Canton and other Chinese coastal cities before Columbus set out on his quest for a shorter and better route to the Indies. By the sixteenth century, commercial value of this traffic with the Orient gave rise to various East Indies companies. England established hers in 1599 which was soon the most powerful of all.

An important part of the cargoes which European merchants and later those from America assembled in Canton was china, especially a porcelain of bluish white cast with Oriental designs delicately brushed on in cobalt blue, gilt, and other colors. The earliest examples were Chinese in shape and decorative feeling. But much as Europeans might admire Oriental products, they had their own ideas about tableware and it was not long before this porcelain took on western shapes and decorations.

59

While the Chinese government accorded European traders scant welcome, the shrewd Cantonese merchants ordered potters in Ching-tê-Chen, a potting city famous from the ninth century, to produce this porcelain, known in its day as East India china, in shapes acceptable to the European trade. Glazed but undecorated, it was then brought overland and by river routes some 500 miles to Canton where the designs were applied in the porcelain-decorating shops.

These designs included monograms, coats of arms, ship decorations, sporting and country scenes, patriotic and fraternal motifs, and sometimes merely a floral medallion with a narrow band of blue enlivened by star-like marks in gold. The usual custom was to send the pattern over by sailing ship with an order for dinner service, tea set, or the like, and in six months or a year it was completed and ready to be put on board another ship for its eventual destination. The whole transaction might take two years.

This East India china was sold to the traders at a ridiculously low price, each piece averaging about a penny. Packed in bales, it was used as ballast for the homeward trip. It brought high prices in the home market, the profit being so great that the long dangerous voyage was a worthwhile risk.

During three hundred years, quantities of this china arrived safely at European and American ports. The high point was reached in the eighteenth century, with American ships joining the traffic-stream bound for Canton during the 1780's. By the turn of the century, our commerce outstripped even that of the powerful English East India Company and some of the Cantonese merchants were advertising in American newspapers.

Typical of the shapes and decoration of this porcelain is the teapot shown in Illustration 67a. Made about 1800, the design is a spurious version of the Arms of the State of New York. In place of the shield between the figures there is a sprig of flowers. Demand for East India china continued to the middle of the nineteenth century, but after 1825 there was less use of European patterns and more of the Chinese motifs. The Fitzhugh pattern (Illustration 67b) is an example of this trend. This soup tureen is part of a large dinner service brought from China between 1830 and 1840. The blue decoration consists of scattered flower and conventional medallions with diapered pattern borders. Other details are entwined branch handles on the lower part and a conventionalized fruit knot on the doomed lid.

The name Oriental Lowestoft is based on an error. In the early days of antique china collecting, East India china became confused with the output of a small, comparatively short-lived pottery in Lowestoft, England. Consequently it was misnamed and, despite various attempts to restore its right name, the misnomer has persisted.

# III

# Glass

THE MAN whose name has long been synonymous with fine antique **glass**
was born in 1729 at Cologne, one of the oldest German glass centers. When
he was twenty-one he sailed for America, landed in Philadelphia, settled in Lancaster County, and by 1752 had married Elizabeth, daughter of Jacob Huber, a
prosperous iron founder with whom he went into business.

It was a profitable venture and had Henry William Stiegel been content
to make stove plates, he could have died wealthy and been completely forgotten.
But he elected to make glass, American glass that could compete with the best
of English and Continental wares then being imported into the colonies. His
glass-making career began in 1763, lasted eleven years during which he built
and managed three glass factories, employed over a hundred and thirty men,
advertised widely, and had distributors in New York, Boston, Baltimore,
Philadelphia, and Eastern Pennsylvania.

His largest glass houses were in Manheim for which he traveled to Europe
to obtain skilled workmen. As a result, his products equaled the best imported
glassware. Nevertheless, the business failed in 1774 and he died ten years
later in obscurity and poverty.

Stiegel is remembered today as the first American glass maker to produce
fine tableware and decorative items commercially. He made three types of blown
glass: colored with quilting (Illustration 68), like the sugar bowl at left,
clear with enameled decoration in colors, like the mug in the center, and clear
with wheel-etched decoration. This last appeared on flip glasses and similar
articles.

Gradually, after his failure, his workmen gravitated to other glass houses
in New York, New England, the Pittsburgh area, and the several factories of
the Ohio Valley, taking with them the Stiegel tradition of color, texture, and
beautiful shape in fine blown glass. Long after Stiegel's death, Stiegel-type
glass continued to be made at these factories by his workmen and their appren-

61

tices. The aquamarine sugar bowl at the right in Illustration 68 is a good example of such glass made in the Middle West, probably at Zanesville, Ohio, about 1800 or later. Some Stiegel-type glass was still being produced as late as 1840.

It is very difficult to distinguish pieces actually made at Manheim from those produced elsewhere in the Stiegel tradition. Also, during the years of the Manheim venture, a considerable amount of fine European glass, like that made by Stiegel, was shipped to America. Consequently, even experts find it safer to use the term, "Stiegel-type," for this glass. Incidentally some fine glass is now being made at Corning, New York, that is of the Stiegel spirit though it of course lacks the irregularities found in examples of the old glass.

### Mold-Blown and Pressed Glass

There seems to be considerable confusion regarding the mold-blown and pressed or pattern types of glass. Possibly this is because both types have two things in common. Both originated as inexpensive substitutes for the fine cut glass imported from England, Ireland, and the continent of Europe. Both were shaped in molds but with a drastic difference of method.

Mold-blown was the earlier type, being in vogue from about 1820 to 1840. Hollow molds made in two, three, or four vertical leaves hinged together were used. These were of iron and the interiors intaglio-cut in designs simulating those of cut glass. When the leaves of such a mold were assembled, the upper end was open and into it was inserted a blowpipe with a gather of hot molten glass. The glass was inflated by the glass blower and quickly took on the shape and design of the mold. Then the mold was opened and the piece still attached to the blowpipe removed. After that it was finished by the usual glass-blowing manipulations. This technique antedated the Christian Era and was extensively used by glass workers of the Roman Empire.

Pressed glass, on the contrary, was a product of the nineteenth century and was the first radical change in glass-making in over two thousand years. Its introduction resulted in a still cheaper imitation of costly cut glass. By this process the red-hot molten glass was pressed into the mold rather than blown. This was accomplished by a plunger affixed to a long lever-like handle which was pressed down on the charge of glass forcing it into the incised design cut in the mold. Then the piece was removed from the mold fully shaped.

While this is the major difference between the mold-blown and pressed glass, there are minor differences: the mold-blown is lighter and thinner; its design in reverse may be felt on the inside and generally there is some trace on the bottom of the piece of where the pontil or handling rod was attached. A piece of pressed glass is heavier and thicker; its inside surface is always smooth and naturally there is no pontil mark on the bottom.

Pressed glass went beyond the aims of the mold-blown in producing a cheap and attractive imitation of cut glass. It revolutionized the glass industry and by the second half of the nineteenth century practically no home was without a good supply of this tableware in varied patterns.

Mold-blown glass, on the other hand, was made for only about thirty years. Originating in Ireland, its manufacture was widespread in the United

States between 1820 and 1850. The technique was probably introduced here by Irish glass blowers who migrated to America during the early years of the century. This glass was produced in quantity by various glass houses in New England, the Pittsburgh area, and Ohio. Some of these factories were short-lived; others eventually turned to the cheaper and more quickly made pressed glass.

Mold-blown was produced mostly in geometric designs, with over five hundred patterns. The objects made include such tableware as plates, goblets, wine glasses, pitchers, celery vases, and decanters, the last being the most common of the pieces that have survived. Other articles were flasks, lamps, inkwells, vases, jars, food holders for bird cages, hats, witch balls, and some miniatures. These were in clear flint glass as well as various shades of green, blue, red, and purple.

Examples in Illustration 69 are all of clear glass and show the variety of objects made as well as the prevalent designs. The early pieces are usually geometric in design but baroque patterns appeared to some extent later. Decanters and water glasses were especially popular, the latter flaring, straight, or barrel-shape as shown in the top and middle rows. Decanters followed the shapes and sizes of the cut-glass ones; the stoppers might be sunburst, hollow knob, or plain like that of the vinegar cruet in the middle row second from the right. Wine glasses, whale oil lamp, hat inkwell, and small pitchers on the bottom row are typical of other pieces in favor at the time. The geometric motifs most commonly used have been given present-day names that are sufficiently descriptive: waffling, ribbing, sunburst, sunburst-in-square, and bull's-eye sunburst. They appear, singly or in combination, in the pieces illustrated.

Mold-blown glass had a definite appeal during the few years of its manufacture, but it was so fragile that examples are now rare and very expensive, indeed far outstripping in value the very cut glass it sought to imitate. Extremely rare are flip glasses, covered sugar bowls, and covered jam dishes with matching plate.

Pressed glass was produced in complete table settings and in various other household accessories for a much longer period than the mold-blown, from 1840 to 1900, and is consequently much more plentiful than the earlier substitute for cut glass.

### Deming Jarves and Lacy Sandwich Glass

Among the types of glass developed in the United States during the early nineteenth century was the well-known lacy Sandwich glass. This highly decorated ware was made in quantity from carefully-cut molds and sold at popular prices. The man responsible for it was Deming Jarves whose factory was opened in 1825 at Sandwich, Massachusetts. Here, in a heavily wooded area on Cape Cod fifty miles from Boston, he founded the Boston & Sandwich Glass Company where the technique of pressed glass was perfected. The glass produced by Jarves was of a quality unexcelled anywhere in the United States and compared favorably with that produced at Baccarat, in France, so renowned for its elaborate glassware.

Three years after its founding, Jarves' company introduced cast glassware with an ornate pattern in relief and a background of fine pinpoint stippling.

This stippling catches the light, producing the silvery lace-like effect that gives the ware its name.

The years of greatest production were between 1828 and 1842. A number of patterns appeared, all with the stippled background which even the best Pittsburgh glass houses could not duplicate. Consequently the name, "Sandwich," became synonymous with first-quality lacy glass. Most Sandwich glass is of the clear flint type, although colored pieces were infrequently manufactured. Deming Jarves was interested in the production of colored glass, and though not a glass blower himself, he carried on many experiments with new tints. The public demand, however, was for the clear glass, so that colored Sandwich is comparatively rare.

Jarves' factory produced many other types of glass, but the lacy glass was unique and the type for which he is best known today. It was apparently intended as an inexpensive substitute for the more costly cut glass. The patterns were numerous and, though they bore little resemblance to those of cut glass, they were so pleasing and the product so reasonable in price that few Victorian households were without at least a few pieces.

It was made in all the forms found on the well-appointed dining tables of the period, from cup plates to trays, compotes, and vegetable dishes. In addition there were individual salt dishes, some cups and saucers, and egg cups.

The patterns were inspired by various sources. Sometimes the design is a combination of geometric motifs so arranged as to simulate fine lace. The floral designs include the rose and thistle, lily, dahlia, tulip and acanthus, and daisy. A pattern of Gothic arches with heart-shaped motifs reflects the influence of the Victorian Gothic revival. Patriotic designs, such as the eagle pattern with thirteen stars, are also found.

Probably the most popular patterns were the heart and leaf, the lyre, and the scrolled peacock's-eye. The rare oblong vegetable dish in Illustration 70, measuring ten by eight and one-half inches and a little over two inches in depth, shows several of these. The scrolled peacock's-eye predominates on the rim and in the center of the dish but the other motifs in the bowl include stylized peacock feathers, lyre, baskets of roses, and thistles.

Lacy Sandwich was made as late as 1850 but as the baroque patterns became more prevalent, the stippled background appeared less often and finally disappeared entirely.

### Bellflower Pattern Glass

American glass factories produced almost five hundred different glass patterns between 1850 and 1890. Collectors, therefore, have a wide choice. Some prefer the early designs of the 1850's pressed in the resonant flint glass which Sandwich and other New England houses favored. Others concentrate on patterns reflecting contemporary American life, such as the Liberty Bell, Westward Ho, and Horseshoe patterns, which were inspired by the Centennial Exposition in Philadelphia.

Among the rare early patterns, Bellflower easily holds first place. Made from about 1855 to 1863, it originated at Sandwich during the later years of Deming Jarves' management. Jarves severed connections with the Boston & Sandwich Glass Company in 1858 but established his Cape Cod Glass

*(Illustration 68)* Stiegel and Stiegel-Type Glass. Left, amethyst quilted sugar bowl; center, mug with enamel decoration in colors; right, pale aquamarine sugar bowl, undecorated.

*(Illustration 69)* American Mold-Blown Glass, ca. 1820-1830.

(*Illustration 70*) Above, Lacy Sandwich Dish, ca. 1828-1842.
(*Illustration 71*) Below, Table Setting of Horseshoe Pattern Glass, ca. 1876.

*(Illustration 72) Bellflower an Early Pattern Glass Rarity.*

(*Illustration 73*) Pittsburgh Glass Made by Bakewell, Pears & Co., ca. 1820-1876.

(*Illustration 74*) American Milk Glass. Compotes are in prism pattern; spoon-holder is loop pattern.

*(Illustration 75)* **Hen-on-Nest Covered Dish of Frosted Glass.**

*(Illustration 76)* American Blown Glass, ca. 1820-1860. Rough pontil mark on bottom of small lamp shown at upper left.

(*Illustration 77*) Tiffany Favrile Glass Bowls. Upper right shows detail of etched mark lettered "L. C. Tiffany–Favrile" and production numbers.

(*Illustration 78*) **Steps in Making Overlay Glass. Left, design outlined; center, cut through white-glass outer layer on grinding wheels; right, after final polishing of facets.**

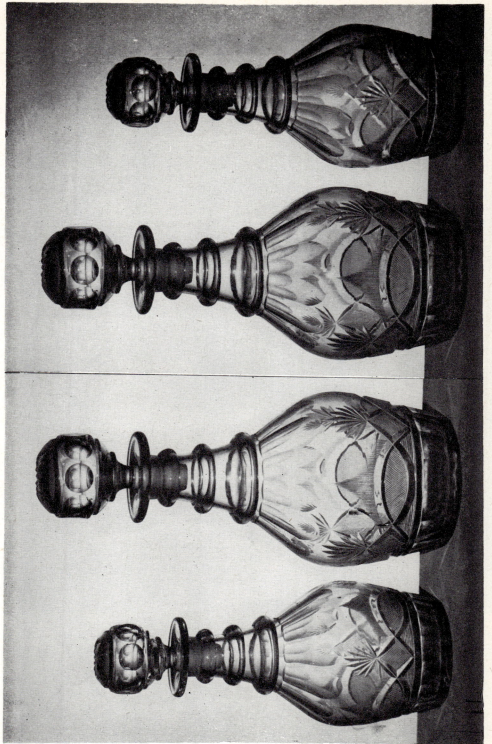

(*Illustration 79*) Set of Irish Cut-Glass Decanters, ca. 1800-1825.

*(Illustration 80)* Typical Millville Rose Paperweight, by Ralph Barber. He made these and others with flower centers in limited numbers from 1905 to 1912. Today they are high priced rarities.

*(Illustration 81)* **American Politics in Glass. Log-cabin and cider-barrel bottles and plates, made for the Harrison-Tyler presidential campaign of 1840.**

*(Illustration 82)* Pattern Glass Goblets with Home-Made Wooden Repairs. In center, an unbroken goblet of similar pattern.

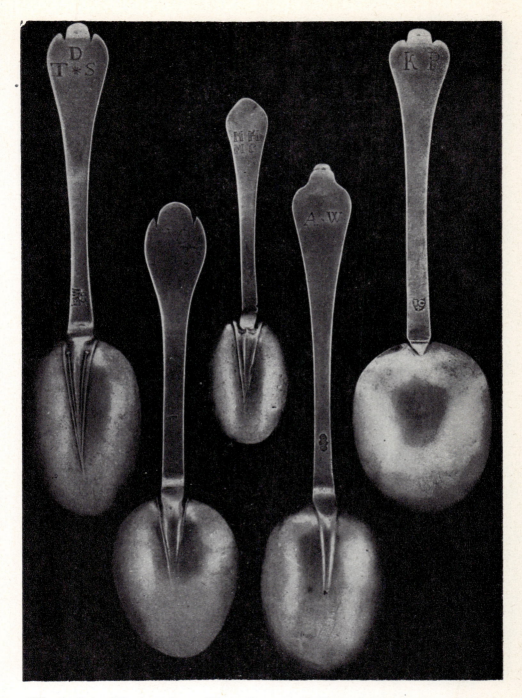

*(Illustration 83)* **American Silver Spoons of Late Seventeenth and Early Eighteenth Centuries. Back-view showing rat-tail decorative detail on bowls and trifid outline of handles, as well as maker's touch-marks.**

*(Illustration 84)* Typical American Silver Spoons, ca. 1790-1850.

Works soon afterward and continued to produce Bellflower, along with other patterns of the period, in both clear and colored glass.

Bellflower was made only of flint glass, but the Cape Cod area was not its sole provenance. Trade catalogues of the late 1880's show pitchers and other ware in this pattern made by M'Kee Brothers of Pittsburgh. However, the general effect of these was more mechanical and considerably less graceful than similar pieces made at Sandwich.

The pieces in Illustration 72 are of clear glass made at Sandwich during the 1850's. The ribbing is delicately executed and the floral design artistically placed. Bellflower itself was not a new decorative motif. It had been popular a half-century before as an inlay design of Hepplewhite and Sheraton furniture, especially that made by Baltimore cabinetmakers. That it lent itself pleasantly to a pattern glass design is shown by this assortment which is part of a well appointed table service in glass of a hundred years ago. Left to right, the pieces are a syrup jug, caster, covered butter dish, high standard covered compote, covered candy jar, goblet, and berry bowl.

Other pieces of the service might include three sizes of bowls, cake plate, celery holder, high standard open compote, cream pitcher, decanters, egg cups, honey dishes, preserve dishes, oval and footed sugar bowls, six-inch plates, water tumblers, whiskey tumblers, and wine glasses. Lamps and mugs were also made in this pattern.

Among the rarities today are covered salt dishes with beaded-edge bases, three-inch honey dishes with scallop and point edge, cake plates on standard, and any dishes in color, especially the sapphire blue favored by Jarves.

### The Centennial and Pattern Glass

The Centennial Exposition, commemorating the one-hundredth anniversary of the signing of the Declaration of Independence, exerted a far-reaching influence on the industrial arts of the United States. After it was announced in 1873 that the financing of this first World's Fair in America had been assured through the sale of one million ten-dollar shares, manufacturers of all kinds began to plan their displays.

Among them were the makers of pattern glass who realized that this Centennial in Philadelphia offered them a profitable opportunity. So, for a year or two before its opening in Fairway Park, pressed-glass factories were very active originating and producing new patterns in glassware. The various companies, especially those of the Ohio River area, located in and around Pittsburgh and at Wheeling, West Virginia, broke away from the styles they had been following for some twenty-five years. Instead of conventionalized motifs, the designers turned to patterns stemming directly from American life.

Between 1875 and continuing for five years or more, some of the definitely American patterns were produced. Among them was the Liberty Bell pattern where the motif was that historical symbol of Independence. In quick succession came the highly prized Westward Ho, and others where domestic, wild or circus animals dominated the design. Along with these, some designers in a glass factory, so far unidentified, originated a pattern in which the horseshoe, traditional symbol of good luck, was the dominating motif.

It occurred in the center of plates and two sizes of platters. On covered pieces, such as sugar bowl, marmalade jar, or compote, the knobs were in the form of standing horseshoes with an anchor in the center (Illustration 71). Salt dishes, large and small, were horseshoe-shaped. The horseshoe does not appear on goblets, wine glasses, creamers, celery vases, or waterpitchers. Instead there is a diagonal stippled panel of small flowers superimposed on the stippled leaves and conventionalized ornaments which accompany the horseshoe motif on the other pieces.

Examples of a table setting in the illustration, left to right, are: top row, goblet, sugar bowl, two wine glasses flanking an open compote, marmalade jar, and creamer; middle row, ten-inch plates at either end, celery vase, covered cheese dish, and water pitcher; bottom row, cake plate on standard that matches stem of wine glasses, oblong dish, large platter lettered "Give us this day our daily bread," oval dish, and covered compote. Other articles in such a setting would include two sizes of salt dishes, finger bowls, spoonholder, and sauce dishes.

From the quantities that have survived, dishes of this pattern must have sold widely. I can remember a small Vermont hotel, located near the entrance to the county fair ground, where sugar bowls, creamers, and other pieces of the Horseshoe pattern were in evidence on a number of the tables. Today the pattern is understandably popular in sections of the country where riding and horse shows play an important part in the social life. Horseshoe is among the patterns that still can be bought at reasonable prices.

### Bakewell, Pears & Company, of Pittsburgh

At the turn of the nineteenth century, the Pittsburgh area was considered a part of the West. It and the Ohio Valley were thickly enough populated for several glass houses to thrive and sell their products nearby. According to a London visitor of 1817, "demand for these articles of elegant luxury lies in the western states, the inhabitants of Eastern America being still importers from the Old Country."

Within a few years the market had expanded from Maine to New Orleans. One of the most important of the glass houses was that of Bakewell, Pears & Co., founded in 1807 by Thomas Bakewell and Benjamin Page, both newly arrived from England. This firm continued in business until 1882, always with some member of the Bakewell family as its head. John Palmer Pears became a partner in 1836.

The firm was famous in its day for its beautiful cut and engraved glass which many connoisseurs considered the equal of the finest European examples. It was also the first to manufacture flint glass successfully. Deming Jarves of Sandwich called Thomas Bakewell "the father of the flint-glass business in this country" in his *Reminiscences of Glass-Making.*

Later, Bakewell's pattern glass rivaled that of Sandwich in quality and design. It also produced a large proportion of the glass bureau knobs that were popular during the American Empire period; it made the first crystal chandelier produced in America in 1810; it made decanters and glasses cut and engraved with the arms of the United States for the White House in 1817; and it made the handsome pair of vases presented to Lafayette during his visit to America in 1825. Within twenty years, this house became the largest flint glass works in America, employing over seventy skilled workers and making practically every type of glass.

The examples in Illustration 73, with the exception of the engraved blown whiskey decanter which dates from about 1820, all belong to the pattern-glass period. The footed covered dishes are in the prism pattern. The cake dish in the center has a "Rebecca-at-the-Well" stem supporting a dish of prism pattern, and dates from the early 1870's. Candlesticks were also produced in this design. Among other designs were the much-imitated dolphin pattern, used for compotes and candlesticks, and the graceful shell design, used particularly for occasional dishes. These both date from the 1850's.

The quantity and variety of glass produced during this firm's seventy-five years of existence was very large and the location of the factory made its distribution comparatively easy. Bakewell glass was shipped via the Ohio and Mississippi Rivers south to Mexico and South America. In Rio de Janeiro, Buenos Aires, and Lima, it is found today and can easily be mistaken for European glass of the best quality.

During the heyday of pattern glass there were several contemporaries of Bakewell, Pears & Co., that produced glassware in large quantities. Some of these were organized by men who had worked earlier at the Bakewell factory. They included Adams & Company, Bryce Brothers, Doyle & Company, George Duncan and Sons, M'Kee Brothers, O'Hara Glass Company, and Ripley & Company.

### Milk Glass versus Porcelain

Knowledge of milk glass goes back to the days of ancient Egypt when it was used for cups and ointment jars as a substitute for alabaster. Roman craftsmen worked with it as early as the beginning of the Christian era, obtaining whiteness by the use of oxide of tin. Sometimes they added a white outer layer to blown colored glass and by cutting through achieved such beautiful cameo effects as in the famous Portland vase.

Then milk glass was forgotten for some fifteen hundred years. In the eighteenth century when European and English potters were searching for the secret of fine Chinese porcelain, milk-glass making was revived by the Venetian glass blowers. Opaque but with a delicate translucence that somewhat resembled china, it was produced in imitation of the more expensive material. Tableware and ornamental objects were blown in the ceramic shapes then in vogue and decorated with gilt and colored enamels in designs similar to those used on fine porcelains.

Between 1750 and the close of the century, milk glass dishes were produced in factories both on the Continent and in England. The English milk glass more successfully duplicates china. That of continental make is often of a bluish-green cast; English-made milk glass, especially that of Bristol, is of a creamy tint. Apparently toward the end of the century there was some effort to court the American market, for an occasional mug or similar object is sometimes found with the patriotic decoration of eagle and stars.

Not until the making of pressed glass in the late 1820's at Sandwich and Cambridge, was any milk glass produced in America. Deming Jarves who introduced this glass at his factory on Cape Cod referred to it as "alabaster glass" and used a formula different than that of the eighteenth-century glass blowers. Where English and European glass metal included tin, the American recipe contained a phosphate and a derivative of magnesia or manganese. With certain combinations an opalescent quality was achieved; with others, a clear white, not unlike certain types of porcelain. At first, small items such as salt dishes and cup plates, were made of this opaque glass. Pressed glass drawer pulls were also made for use on American Empire chests of drawers and desks.

As the nineteenth century progressed, candlesticks, lamp bases, tableware, and small novelty dishes with animal or fowl covers were made of milk glass. The high point, both in quantity production and variety of patterns, came in the 1850's. It was then that milk-white dinner services were turned out by pressed glass makers in various sections of the country.

Decorative effect was achieved by mold patterns rather than by the colored enamels that had characterized English and European milk glass of the preceding century. In Illustration 74, the two covered sweetmeat dishes, attributed to M'Kee Brothers of Pittsburgh, are fine examples of the prism pattern. Another popular design was the loop pattern of which the spoon holder in the center is an example. This piece is opalescent in tone. Both patterns were in vogue during the 1850's. Plates with openwork rims date from the latter part of the century.

There seems to have been no conscious attempt to imitate contemporary china. American pattern glass was a substitute tableware. The opaque or milk white was just another form of a ware that was even cheaper to manufacture than earthenware and lent itself to an endless number of pleasing patterns.

### Birds and Beasts of Glass

Bird and animal motifs were common throughout the Victorian period and appeared in various forms, from the cast-iron deer on well-kept lawns to the embroidered antimacassars on the armchairs inside the house. Among the articles most popular at the time and prized today by collectors were covered glass dishes in the shape of birds and animals. These date from the latter part of the Victorian era and were for the most part made in and around Pittsburgh.

The idea was not new. Covered porcelain dishes representing animals originated in China and were later made in Europe at the Dresden factory and by the potters of Staffordshire. Such dishes were popular in America from about 1790 to 1820 but were too expensive to be in general use. In the 1870's several glass factories in the midwest began making a covered dish in the form of a hen on a nest (Illustration 75). These dishes, manufactured in pressed glass, were turned out in quantity and sold for as little as ten cents for one of small size. They were commonly made in three sizes—three, five, and seven inches being the length of the nest.

The design proved such a great success that pattern-glass manufacturers introduced other bird and animal forms. Roosters and farm animals are listed as a "Farmyard Assortment" in trade catalogues of the period, although such unlikely subjects as swans, fish, and eagles were included. A duck and a robin were among those current in the 1880's, as well as dogs, cats, rabbits, lambs, horses, and finally, after the domestic scene was exhausted, lions and other wild beasts.

Of them all, the hen on the nest remained the favorite and continues so today. A close second was the duck which was also made by a number of western glasshouses, among them the Atterbury Glass Company, M'Kee Brothers, United States Glass Company, all of Pittsburgh, and the Central Glass Company of Wheeling, West Virginia, where the hen on nest in Illustration 75 was made in the 1880's. Known as a covered egg dish, this seven-inch example was filled with a dozen fresh bantam eggs and given in 1885 as a wedding present to a young school teacher in Vermont by the grandmother of one of her pupils. It has been the prized possession of her family for over seventy years and is still without nick or chip, perhaps because for the first fifty years it was used only once a year—for the traditional boiled eggs of the Easter breakfast.

These dishes were also made in clear glass, in opalescent white and satin finish, in turquoise, olive green, caramel, and opaque blue. Sometimes the hen or rooster is opalescent white, hand-painted in naturalistic colors, while the nest is straw-colored. They were originally intended as table accessories—the largest for boiled or scrambled eggs, the smallest for condiments or sweetmeats. From the latter use doubtless came the idea of selling them to the manufacturers of mustard and spices as fancy containers for their products. Many of these premium items were in milk glass and opaque blue.

Although covered glass dishes in animal forms were mass-produced, they were so attractive that they have survived where many a more costly piece has not. The hen on the nest is still being made but both the design and the workmanship of the modern pieces lack the charm of the old examples.

### American Blown Glass of the Nineteenth Century

Glassware of a century ago was not all of the pressed-pattern type. Pressed glass was the ordinary ware for everyday use; for special occasions, the ware chosen was apt to be blown glass.

Consequently, among the heirlooms of most old households there are usually a number of pieces similar to those in Illustration 76. Since so much emphasis has been placed on Stiegel-type and other rare glass of the eighteenth century, it is difficult to assign a place to these simple nineteenth-century pieces in the history of American glass.

The approximate age of a piece can often be judged by its design and general appearance. The place of its manufacture usually remains in question unless the original owner was methodical enough to preserve a bill of sale. The paneled goblet in the center is one of a set long believed to have been made in Cork, Ireland. Subsequent discovery of the bill for them from a Boston agent, dated 1852, identified them as products of the New England Glass Company of Cambridge, Massachusetts.

It is frequently difficult to tell whether a given piece is American-made or imported, especially since many of our best glass factories made a practice of inducing skilled craftsmen from Europe and Great Britain to work for them. The New England Glass Company, for example, employed many English and Irish glass blowers. The paneled design of goblet was obviously a popular one between 1840 and 1850. Not long ago I was able to find six that matched mine at a local antique show.

The whale-oil lamp at the extreme left is a very simple piece, made about 1820, probably at one of the smaller New England glass houses. It has a very rough pontil mark on the bottom, shown in the insert above. This sure indication of blown glass ranges in appearance from a rough swirl to a smooth polished depression, depending on the care in finishing a piece.

The sillabub or Madeira glass next to it is well formed and finished but the pontil mark is not ground away. It dates from before 1840 and is typical of many produced in America at the time.

The goblet and the trumpet vase both have the button-like depression showing the pontil mark ground and polished as was usual with fine pieces. The trumpet vase shows the influence of the Bohemian glass workers who were employed in several American glass houses. The grape leaf and tendril etching was a favored motif for the ruby glass of Bohemia, so much prized during the Victorian period. This vase, made about 1860, was found in Brooklyn, New York, and may have been made at one of the glass houses in existence there at the time.

### Favrile Glass

Unusual coloring and finish were characteristics of ornamental or "art glass" production in the United States between 1880 and 1930. Fashioning of such decorative pieces as bowls, vases, and candlesticks called for superior glass-making skills. Outstanding among these late art forms of glass is that known as Favrile, a name chosen by its inventor, Louis Comfort Tiffany, from an old Saxon word meaning "hand wrought."

For the glass enthusiast, favrile is an ideal subject to collect since every piece is clearly marked on the base in acid-etched lettering. This reads either "L. C. T. Favrile" or, after 1900, "L. C. Tiffany-Favrile." Production of it began in 1883 and ended in 1930 when Mr. Tiffany at the age of 81 destroyed all the formulas for its making.

The delicate coloring of classic Greek and Roman glass that had become iridescent from being buried in tombs since the beginning of the Christian Era was the inspiration for this glass. Louis Comfort Tiffany was the artistic son of Charles L. Tiffany, founder of the famous New York firm of jewelers. Louis was an accomplished painter and also head of the decorating branch of the family business known as The Tiffany Studios, which executed many important commissions, especially for churches.

Stained glass windows stimulated Mr. Tiffany's interest and, in 1883, he established his factory at Corona, New York, to make iridescent glass for use in such windows. Manned by a group of expert glass workers from Stourbridge, England, it was at first known as the Stourbridge Glass Company and shortly afterward as The Tiffany Furnaces.

Louis Tiffany did not intend to make his glass works a commercial enterprise and at first limited production to single pieces as works of art. Many of these made during the first decade of the factory's existence are now in collections of important museums in America and Europe. Gradually, favrile glass began to appear in many forms—trumpet vases, footed and plain bowls of various sizes, candlesticks, delicate wine glasses, and other decorative accessories, even including shades and bowls for electric-light fixtures.

It was this commercialization of favrile glass that caused its originator to buy back the stock of his principal assistants, to close the plant, and destroy the thousands of formulas developed during the nearly fifty years of the Tiffany glass enterprise. For a few years some of the men who worked in the Tiffany glass house tried to produce glass of the same type, but it was never the same. It lacked the unique depth of color and sheen of the original.

Iridescence is the dominant characteristic of all Tiffany favrile glass. The usual colors are peacock blue, burnished gold, and Nile green. The two latter have more translucence than those of peacock blue and are sometimes further enhanced with flower and leaf decoration. The iridescence was achieved by the fumes of various metal and metal-oxide solutions used in thousands of combinations.

According to tradition, Mr. Tiffany visited his glass works each morning and personally inspected what had come from the annealing lehrs the previous day. Those pieces which he felt were not of Tiffany quality, he let crash to the floor as they were handed to him, in the manner of the great potter, Wedgwood.

Of the two examples in Illustration 77, the large bowl at the left, nine and three-quarter inches in diameter, is a rich iridescent blue and bears the mark "L. C. T. Favrile" on the bottom, indicating that it dates from before 1900. The small footed bowl at the right, made about 1915, is of burnished gold shading to peacock blue at the base. It is marked "L. C. Tiffany-Favrile". Upper right shows a typical mark with production numbers.

### Overlay Glass

Although the technique of overlay glass dates back to Roman days, its popularity in the modern world dates from the Victorian era. Extensive production of this glass originated in Bohemia, spreading later to France, Belgium, and England.

A certain amount was exported to America, but not until the New York Crystal Palace Exhibition of 1853 did our glassmakers take any great interest in it. An impressive showing of French and Bohemian glass articles created a demand that reached its peak during the 1860's. Probably the factories at Sandwich and Cambridge were the first in America to make this kind of glass.

These factories often hired foreign glass blowers to teach their workers such techniques as were necessary to compete with the European product. Lamps of the kerosene type which had superseded the earlier whale-oil lamp were the articles most frequently made of overlay glass. American factories also made a variety of other objects, such as decorative glass for Victorian front doors, vases, carafes, perfume and cologne bottles, and miniature glass hats. Dorflinger of New York made the hats even after the turn of the twentieth century.

The beauty of overlay glass lay in the skill with which the cutter executed the design from a blown blank. Over clear or colored glass a contrasting shell was applied while the whole was white hot. Then came a reheating to fuse the two layers. After proper annealing, it went to the grinding and polishing department where a pattern was cut through the outer shell to reveal the glass of another color beneath it. In Illustration 78, the successive steps in executing the pattern on a lamp font are readily seen. Left, the design is drawn in outline; center, the design is cut through the layer of milk-white glass to the ruby-red glass beneath; right, the finished object is ground and polished.

Overlay lamps, though popular, were never cheap. With simple types the overlay was confined to the font. Stems and bases might be of brass and marble or of different kinds of glass. Such lamps are from ten to fourteen inches high. Larger and more elaborate ones have bowls and stems of overlay glass cut in intricate patterns and are from twenty-one to thirty-eight inches high.

Overlay lamps are popular today with collectors since they can be easily electrified for use in the modern home. Reproductions have appeared on the market but a good observer can usually detect them by the thin overlay on the bowl and the newness of brass collar. They are usually smaller than the Victorian lamp.

### Irish Cut Glass

The art of glass cutting came to England from the Continent about 1720. However, it did not flourish as an Act of Parliament of 1746 taxed glass according to weight of metal. This duty did not hold in Ireland but the Act forbade exportation of glass from there. Consequently, glass heavy enough to stand cutting was not made extensively in either country. The Act was partially repealed in 1780, leaving a tax for English glass but none for that made in Ireland.

The advantage of the latter was such that glass houses producing cut glass were soon erected in Waterford, Cork, Dublin, and Belfast. Workmen, tools, and materials were imported from England. From then until the middle of the nineteenth century, the manufacture of cut glass was a lively Irish industry with quantities exported to the United States, particularly from the cutting shops of Waterford and Cork.

Since the workmen there were English-trained, designs, forms, and other features differed practically not at all from those produced in English factories. The first workmen at Waterford came from Stourbridge and the glass made was naturally Stourbridge but of Waterford provenance. Furthermore, this factory used a design book, entitled *English, Irish, and Scotch Patterns*, from about 1820 to 1830. Also the habit the glass workers had of moving from one shop to another makes it almost impossible to tell whether old cut glass originated in Ireland, England, or America. Quantities of fine cut glass were produced in the latter during these years by Bakewell, Pears of Pittsburgh, the New England Glass Company at Cambridge, and by many others.

On the body of the decanters (Illustration 79), the pointed ovals alternating with lozenges, both finely crosscut, were a favorite Waterford motif. The fans and arched fringe elements were used on both Cork and Waterford pieces. But the variety of patterns using one or more of these motifs was so great and access to them so universal that, unless one's forebears were considerate enough to have preserved an identifying bill of sale, the provenance of a piece is very difficult to ascertain.

The original owners of these decanters always referred to them as "Irish decanters." Since such glass was imported and sold in America in quantity from 1786 to about 1830, the origin of these four pieces is probably Waterford, or possibly Cork.

As for the technique of glass cutting, it is and always has been done in four successive stages, whether carried out by the individual Irish cutter in his cottage or by four different specialists in a large factory. First, the design to be cut is marked on the plain piece, or blank. Then iron wheels, kept moist with a mixture of fine sand and water, cut the deeper elements of the design. Stone disks refine the major cuttings and add the smaller lines and motifs. Lastly comes the polishing with rapidly revolving wooden disks onto which is fed a fine stream of moist powdered rotten-stone and pumice.

### Millville Rose Paperweights

The glass paperweight known as the Millville Rose had for its origin a technique probably first used by the old Venetian glass workers. It was that of embedding a pattern of colored glass within a casing of clear glass. The process became known in other parts of Europe and was finally introduced in America by the skilled craftsmen imported by such glass houses as Sandwich and Cambridge in the second half of the nineteenth century.

It has long been the custom of the individual glass worker to use the left-over glass in the pot at the end of the day to fashion pieces for his own amusement. The workers in the factory of Whitall, Tatum, & Company, at Millville, New Jersey, makers of chemical and pharmaceutical glassware, were experimenting with the making of paperweights in their free time as early as the 1880's. They even created a paperweight with a rose motif, but this was quite unlike the paperweight with the standing rose design which came to be known as the Millville Rose.

The Millville Rose paperweights were the creation of four glass workers: Ralph Barber, Emil Stanger, Marcus Kuntz, and John Rhulander. All were excellent craftsmen but Ralph Barber was the foremost. After six years of experimentation with colored glass for the rose, he found the right type at a factory in Brooklyn which permitted the standing full-blown rose to be annealed without cracking.

The four men not only made these paperweights as gifts but also produced them to sell as a private venture. Barber continued to make them after the others had withdrawn, his years of production being from about 1905 to 1912. He lived until 1936 and had the unusual experience of seeing his rose paperweights, originally priced at $1.50 each, command as much as $500 for a single fine example.

Barber modeled his roses with opalescent tips to the petals which are always shown fully open. The blooms vary from a rich red to a delicate pink. The finest and rarest are those accompanied by a bud and a leaf, as in Illustration 80. He also produced some of canary yellow, green, or other shades which resulted accidently from the high annealing temperatures. In addition to his roses, he made some weights with other motifs: calla lilies, water lilies, and tulips. In all of these, the flower is represented in full bloom.

Barber's paperweights are completely different from those of any other

73

glass craftsman. Although they were a product of their maker's spare time, since his regular work was the manufacture of special glassware for druggists and laboratories, these flower paperweights are unique and still defy reproduction.

## Early American Politics in Glass

In addition to their personal and sentimental interest, there are certain heirlooms which have added appeal because they mirror important happenings of their day. In glass there are such examples as the rare Constitution cup plate which was made at Sandwich in 1830 and reflected the furor of public interest that followed publication of Oliver Wendell Holmes' poem, "Old Ironsides"; the Jenny Lind flasks, celebrating the spectacular tour of the "Swedish Nightingale" here in 1850 as staged by the showman, P. T. Barnum; the Flora Temple flask, blown in 1860 after this mid-nineteenth century star of the race track had defeated the favorite, George W. Patchen, in a trotting match at Union Course on Long Island.

Political events also influenced glass design. During the campaign of 1840, many pieces were produced to promote the cause of the Whig candidates, General William Henry Harrison and Governor John Tyler, who without a party platform defeated Martin VanBuren for reelection.

With the slogan "Tippecanoe and Tyler Too," the Whigs made campaign capital of the charge that their standard bearer was a backwoods pioneer who lived in a log cabin, wore a coonskin cap, and drank hard cider. Demand for "a change" took the place of any policy declaration and, by the time the campaign got well under way, practically every hamlet had its log cabin with cider barrel by the doorway. The fact that General Harrison was a gentleman farmer living in a handsome mansion at North Bend on the Ohio, just north of Cincinnati, and was addicted neither to coonskin caps nor hard cider, was completely overlooked.

American glass factories turned out bottles, flasks, drinking glasses, bowls, plates, and other articles decorated with the Whig campaign emblems. They must have been produced in quantity but, like present-day campaign buttons, few have survived. Among those found are two types of flasks, one design of the log cabin bottle, another in the form of a cider barrel, a few bowls, and some plates.

The flasks are rare. One has a slightly raised decoration of a log cabin and the words "Tippecanoe" and "North Bend." The other type (Illustration 81) is of greenish glass with a log cabin on one side and on the reverse a fluttering American flag, a barrel, a plow, and the words "Hard Cider." The log cabin bottle has a front and rear door with "Tippecanoe" over one and "Harrison" over the other. The small barrel-shaped bottle has "Hard Cider" on one side and "Tippecanoe Extract" on the other in raised letters. It was probably used for applejack.

The "Industry" plate, so called because of its border motifs, may have originated at Sandwich. In the center is the usual log cabin with front door open and the ever-present barrel at the left-hand side. In the stippled background border are four scenes, two of a man plowing, one of a factory, and one of a square rigged ship with all sails set, emblematic of commerce and industry. Such plates were made with both scalloped and plain edges. Those with scalloped edges are rarer and more desirable today. Small bowls were also produced in this same design.

At least eleven varieties of Harrison-Tyler cup plates are known. Two have profile portraits of Harrison in the center and another, without inscription, is known to have been made at Sandwich. Nine have a log cabin. One bears the inscription, "Fort Meigs" to commemorate Harrison's defense of it in 1812, also "Tippecanoe" and his name.

It is not known who paid for these various campaign objects in glass. But whether the costs came out of Whig campaign funds or whether partisans paid gladly for these symbols that proved so effective, these mementos of past political contests today command high prices.

### A Unique Repair of Broken Goblets

All who have antiques about their homes are faced at one time or another with the repair problem. A favorite possession is broken or damaged. Can it be repaired? Will the result be worth the expense? Might the owner do it himself? Generally, except for collectors who have well-equipped workshops, genuine skill, and an ability to do work of professional quality, it is advisable to have the work done by a specialist. With a piece of furniture, a good cabinet-maker can usually repair an injured piece so well that only careful examination will disclose what has been done. The same holds with silver or pewter. China specialists accomplish wonders with their rivets, cements, and touch-up enamels.

Broken glass of course cannot be made whole again nor can cracks be eradicated. But, where a piece has a slight chip on the rim, the glass repair specialist can remove it by grinding and repolishing. Replacement stoppers for decanters can also be ground to fit. If the stem of a goblet, compote, or vase is broken, a well-fitted silver ferrule is the solution.

With all these it is assumed that the piece is important enough to warrant the expense of repair. The silver ferrule would hardly be worth while for an odd piece, but would be proper for one of a pair or of a table setting of blown or pattern glass. In the past, pattern glass would not have been considered worth while to repair as it was cheap, expendable ware. When goblet stems were broken, the footless drinking glasses were relegated for common use at well or spring or to the cemetery as flower holders.

There sometimes was an exception, however, as shown by two goblets with wooden bases (Illustration 82). They were done about a hundred years ago by some thrifty and ingenious Yankee who had a sense of line and proportion. The wooden bases are eight-sided and flaring for stability. He refined the design of one by adding a slightly raised band at the bottom. They are made of soft wood, one pine and the other spruce. The broken stem of the goblet was inserted in a large hole filled with common putty. When after some weeks this hardened, the owner once more had two usable goblets and their repair had cost him nothing.

Was his motive thrift or were the glasses part of a set of twelve that for family reasons were of sentimental value? They are of the Bigler pattern, a pressed glass made at Sandwich and other larger glass factories from 1840 to 1860. Their original glass stems would be similar to the perfect goblet in Flute pattern (center). Both were a variation of Ashburton, one of the first of the pattern designs.

# IV

# Silver

*Rare American Silver Spoons*

I T SEEMS UNLIKELY today that clearly marked spoons by American silversmiths of the seventeenth or eighteenth centuries should be found in an old shoe box with an assortment of much later and very battered silver. But that is just what happened only a few years ago when two spoons, nearly as old as those in Illustration 83, were so found. Fortunately, most people who buy old silver as scrap metal know enough about the marks of silversmiths to sort out such pieces before the balance is sent to an assayer to be melted down as scrap metal. But there is always the chance that fine old pieces may go unappreciated to the melting pot. Hence the importance of studying the marks on spoons and knowing what they mean.

The spoons here illustrated are the work of five silversmiths who lived between 1645 and 1753. Spoons of this period have distinct style characteristics. The bowls are either egg-shaped or oval, usually with a raised and tapered ornamental device on the back known as a "rat-tail." The handles end in either a trifid, like the spoon at the right and the two at the left, or in a cartouche, the second from the right and center.

Spoons range in size from the condiment to the tablespoon. Teaspoons are the most numerous, the early ones being very small. The silversmith's touchmark is usually found on the back of the handle a short distance from where it joins the bowl, or it may be on the inside of the bowl. This mark is often two initials, especially on early examples, but may be initial and surname. Incidentally, "J" is always written "I," as may be noted with these particular spoons where the Christian name of three out of the five makers begins with a "J."

The spoon on the right bears the mark "IC" in a heart-shape with fleur-de-lis below and is that of John Coney, a Boston silversmith, who lived from 1656 to 1722. His contemporary, Jeremiah Dummer, also of Boston (1645-1718), made the condiment spoon in the center and put his mark "ID" on the inside of the bowl. These initials may be in a small rectangle

76

or in a heart with fleur-de-lis below. At the left of the condiment spoon is a teaspoon by Jacob Boelen of New York (1654-1729). His mark is partially worn away but still shows part of a shield with initials "IB." Single teaspoons by these three men have sold at auction at from $300 to $500. The two remaining examples have brought somewhat less. The second spoon from the right, bearing the mark "N. HURD" in a rectangle, was made by Nathaniel Hurd of Boston (1729-1777), a well-known and highly regarded craftsmen in his time and with collectors today. The spoon at the extreme left which bears the touch-mark of Edward Winslow of Boston (1669-1753), brought less than one hundred dollars at auction a few years ago. Ironically, a sweet-meat dish bearing his mark "EW" in shield with fleur-de-lis below was considered fine enough in his day to be sent as a gift to England where it compared favorably with the best work of London craftsmen.

### Sixty Years of Silver Spoons

From the Middle Ages on, the silver spoon has been a symbol of a certain standard of living. "Born with a silver spoon in his mouth," has long indicated a person who began life shielded from the harsh winds of poverty. Silver spoons were among the first investments made by English yeomen or the early American colonists to mark a change in their social status as they struggled up from meager beginnings.

Gifts of silver spoons also marked such important events as births, weddings, and deaths. In the American colonies from the 1640's, when the first spoons were hammered out, to the middle of the nineteenth century, when mechanized production forced the silversmith out of business, silver spoons were part of a young woman's dowry. The quantity depended on the family's financial position, but it was a poverty-stricken household that could not find the money for at least six teaspoons and a tablespoon or two.

Although silver-spoon making goes back at least to the twelfth century, most of those still suitable for use date from between 1780 and 1850. Earlier examples are in museums or private collections. Even spoons made during the first half of the eighteenth century are none too plentiful.

The reason is obvious. Although spoons were made in fair quantity from the time of John Hull in the seventeenth century, constant use took its toll. Furthermore, there was the practice of melting down old silver to appear again in newer designs which continued until well into the nineteenth century. The examples in Illustration 84 are representative of what one might conceivably expect to find among one's heirlooms.

The types that preceded them in the second half of the seventeenth century were first a rounded bowl with a hexagonal handle; then came the rat-tail, so-called because of a projection on the back of its bowl, which was elliptical in shape. With the 1700's, there was a narrower bowl and a less flattened stem, and by 1750 handle tips and bowls became more pointed.

Thus, in the spoon on the extreme left whose maker worked in Philadelphia about 1793, we have the slender handle with pointed end. Bright-cutting, a popular form of ornamentation, appears on the next spoon, New York-made in the 1800's. The third spoon has the "coffin-lid" handle and may have been given to relatives and friends of the deceased instead of the usual mourning ring of the day; but probably it is so-named merely because of the shape. The fourth spoon, made in the 1790's, is by Thomas Revere, brother of Paul. The fifth, with shell-shaped bowl, is one of the novelty spoons designed for sugar. From the shape of its handle, known as "fiddle-back," it might date from anytime in the 1840's. A contemporary and rarer shape is that of the shovel. This may reflect the beginning of public works and building of the early railroads. The doll's spoon at the top was also made about 1850 or slightly later. These miniature spoons were the work of apprentices and were tests of their skill. Spoons with handles like the shell or shovel sugar spoons are late but artistic in outline.

### American Antique Silver, Marked and Unmarked

Practically all antique American silver, the work of craftsmen who plied their trade for better than two centuries, is marked. The touch marks at first were one or two initials, sometimes with a small device added. Later, from about 1760 to 1870, many silversmiths used their surnames, with or without initials.

In England such marking was required by law. In the American colonies and later the United States, no silversmith was legally bound to impress what he made with either symbol or name. They did it rather from pride in their work which settled beyond question what pieces were the products of each silversmithing shop.

Nevertheless, pieces do turn up on which no mark can be found. With some, there are faint indications of a mark, erased by use and polishing. Others bear no indication that they were ever marked.

The owner of a marked piece of silver is fortunate. With the help of one of the several books of check lists of known American silversmiths, he can determine the approximate age and provenance of his piece. Such lists give names, dates, and localities, compiled from all kinds of records. Consequently, the owner can acquire definite information that may materially increase the market value of his piece.

For instance, the two silver cream pitchers in Illustration 85 are practically identical except for size. Both were made about 1760. The one at the left is unmarked; the other bears the touch mark "J. Coburn" on the base. A check list soon determines that the maker was John Coburn of Boston who lived from 1725 to 1803. He was a prolific silversmith, his silver being well known to collectors and bringing good prices. When auctioned several years ago, this small pitcher brought $225. The slightly larger but unmarked pitcher, beautifully made and of the same period, brought only one hundred dollars. An obviously antique, pear-shaped piece with scroll handles, short legs, and leaf-shaped feet, typical of pre-Revolutionary years, it will serve just as well for cream as the one by Coburn, but lack of a mark reduced its price by over half.

Fine unmarked pieces offer the collector an opportunity to gather excellent silver at bargain prices, provided he knows American silver sufficiently well to date examples by shape and workmanship. For example, I saw a silver porringer of no later date than 1800 auctioned for fifty dollars merely because it bore no mark or trace of one. It would have brought more than double had it borne the touch of a recorded silversmith. Again, while a bobbin-shaped pitcher bearing the mark of Paul Revere can bring as much as $2,500, his work always bringing much higher prices than equally well-designed pieces by other contemporary craftsmen, an unmarked piece can be acquired for a tenth of that price, or even less.

### Old and Not-So-Old Silver

The question of age is usually the first to arise in a discussion of old silver. If the given article is English, its hall-marks will give the answer, even to the year. If American, the matter is not so simple. Three pieces of varying ages are here illustrated to demonstrate some of the points by which old and not-so-old silver may be recognized (Illustration 86).

At a quick glance the miniature cream pitcher at the left would seem to have been made about the close of the eighteenth century. Shape and ribbed decoration, known as gadrooning, are of the years between 1790 and 1820, loosely called Later Georgian in classifying English silver. A look on the bottom at the hall-mark identifies the piece as a twentieth-century reproduction. The marks are the initials "H.M." for the maker, an anchor for the place, Birmingham, a lion passant indicating the English standard of fineness, and the letter "I" for the date, 1908-09. A hundred or more years might, quite innocently, get added to this piece. Though not quite fifty years old, it is in Georgian style and at least partially handmade. But even though it is not an antique, its owner can still admire and use it with pleasure.

On the other hand, a piece of silver sometimes has more years to its credit than family tradition would give it. Such is the story of the mug at the right. The date, 1854, is part of the inscription, done when the mug was given as a christening present to an infant in Vermont. The handsome repoussé work on its body and the ornate handle date it around 1850 when such ornamentation was done by Hammond & Company of New York, silversmiths. The mug had originally been a beaker of twelve-ounce capacity, made by an earlier New York silversmith, Myer Myers (1723-1795).

Once handleless and unadorned, save for shaping and simple beading top and bottom, it shared the fate of much old silver in being brought up to date nearly a century later. The almost obliterated touch mark "MM" of its original maker was only discovered a few years ago. The mug's value as an antique was of course considerably lessened by the added ornamentation, but even that was done a long time ago. A little large for a child's drinking cup, it was a spoon holder during the silver-napkin-ring era. Now it is one of the show pieces in a corner cupboard.

The center piece is a small bowl of Sheffield plate, dating from the late eighteenth century. It was part of a bachelor's service, so-called because used by young men of fashion in London who could afford two-room quarters in a good neighborhood with a manservant to attend them. This Sheffield plate service probably corresponded to the "place setting" advertised by fine china shops today. The bowl is unmarked as is frequently the case since the makers of Sheffield plate were not bound by the rules of the Assay Company, but shape, style, and signs of wear date it. Today, this small bowl makes a good container for sugar. Over the years the original plating of silver has nearly disappeared, showing the soft warm sheen of copper beneath. It is a matter of personal taste whether it should be left as is or replated by the modern method.

### Myer Myers, Famous New York Silversmith

Although silversmiths in the other colonies of eighteenth-century America followed English forms and styles closely, those of New York were influenced first by the Dutch and then later by the English. The result was a style combining both Dutch and English features. The workers were of varied national strains—Dutch, English, French, and occasionally Hebrew.

Myer Myers (1723-1795) was a Hebrew and an outstanding silversmith. His working years covered over half a century and during it he produced a quantity of silver ranging from tankards to teaspoons. He maintained a good-sized shop with several journeyman, was a prominent Mason, and in 1776 was elected president of the New York Silversmiths Society.

In addition to tankards, coffee pots, teapots, beakers, and other household wares, he produced fine ecclesiastical pieces for both synagogues and churches. None of his silver was ornate. His only oncession to the prevailing rococo fashion was the scroll-molded spout and cone finial on some of his coffee pots. A tankard made in 1750 for Daniel Shelton of Stratford, Connecticut, is a good example of his restraint in decorative detail (Illustration 87). The plain cylindrical shape tapers from a molded base to a low domed cover which has a scalloped frontal chased with leaf scrolls. There is a scrolled thumbpiece decoration on the strap handle which ends in a heart-shaped pendant. A monogram is engraved on the center of the cover, "D.S." for the original owner. The engraved initials "J.S." were added when the piece passed to his daughter, Jane. The maker's touch mark, "Myers," occurs on the bottom of the tankard and once on the inside of the cover. This piece was owned by three generations of the Shelton family and then was sold at auction for $1,250.

Like a number of other American silversmiths, Myer Myers had several touch marks. They are "MM" in Roman capitals joined in a lozenge; "MM" in script in a rectangle; "Myers" in script in a lozenge; and "Myers" in italics in a rectangle.

A fair amount of Myers silver is still in existence. When it has been left in its original state it eagerly sought by silver collectors. Some of it has unfortunately been tampered with — a spout added to convert a tankard into a teapot, or a plain beaker dressed up with Victorian repoussé design and a handle added. Such transformations undoubtedly gave great pleasure to owners of old silver at the time since the result was a handsome up-to-date piece, but today the value of such a piece is only a quarter of what it would have been had it been left as it came from the shop of Myer Myers.

### Paul Revere, Patriot and Silversmith

For a full century the *Boston News Letter* carried advertisements of the silversmithing business of Paul Revere, father and son. The elder, christened Apollos Rivoire, was born in 1702 on the Isle of Guernsey of Huguenot parents. When only a lad of thirteen he arrived in America, landing in Boston where he was apprenticed to the leading silversmith and engraver of the first paper money used in the Colonies, John Coney (1650-1722).

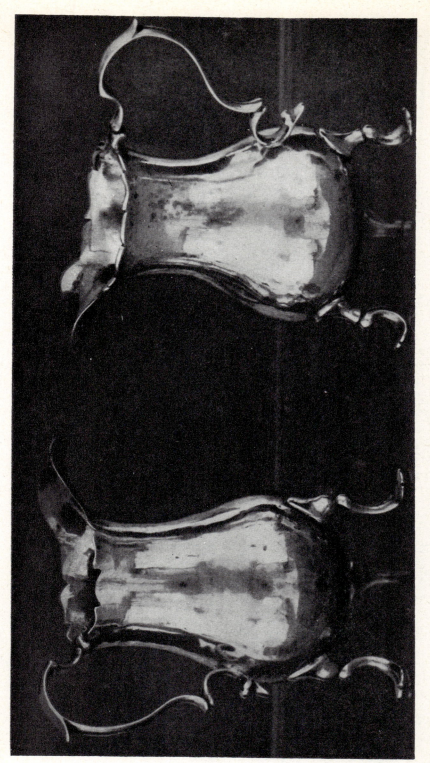

*(Illustration 85)* American Silver Pear-Shaped Cream Pitchers, ca. 1760.

(*Illustration 86*) **Present Day, Eighteenth and Nineteenth-Century Silver. Left,** copy of a Georgian English creamer; center, small Sheffield plate bowl, ca. 1790; right, American mug, dated 1854.

(*Illustration 87*) Silver Tankard, by Myer Myers, ca. 1750.

*(Illustration 88)* Classic Silver Sugar Bowl, by Paul Revere, ca. 1790.

*(Illustration 89)* A Paul Revere Silver Spoon. The back shows his mark, "REVERE," in an oblong at center of handle.

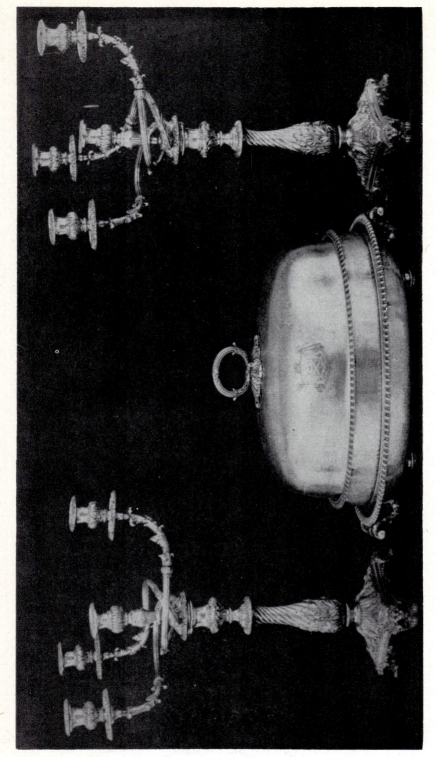

(*Illustration 90*) Sheffield Plate Candlesticks and Domed Platter, ca. 1790-1830.

(*Illustration 91*) American Electroplated Coffee Service, ca. 1865. Maker's label shown in insert, upper right.

*(Illustration 92)* **London Silver for Eighteenth-Century Americans. Lighthouse coffee pot, by Paul Lamerie, London 1729, and four cast silver candlesticks, London 1716, but lacking maker's touch-mark.**

*(Illustration 93)* Bateman Silver in Classic Adam Designs. Left, Hester Bateman teapot, London 1783. Right, sugar urn, London 1817, by son Peter and daughter Ann.

(*Illustration 94*) "Husking," Rated as Currier & Ives' Finest Print. Done from Eastman Johnson's painting, "Cornhusking."

(*Illustration 95*) "Home To Thanksgiving," by Currier & Ives after the painting by Durrie.

*The Old Print Shop*

(*Illustration 96*) "New England Winter Scene." Currier & Ives print after the painting by Durrie.

(*Illustration 97*) *Witch of the Waves*, a Small-Folio Print.

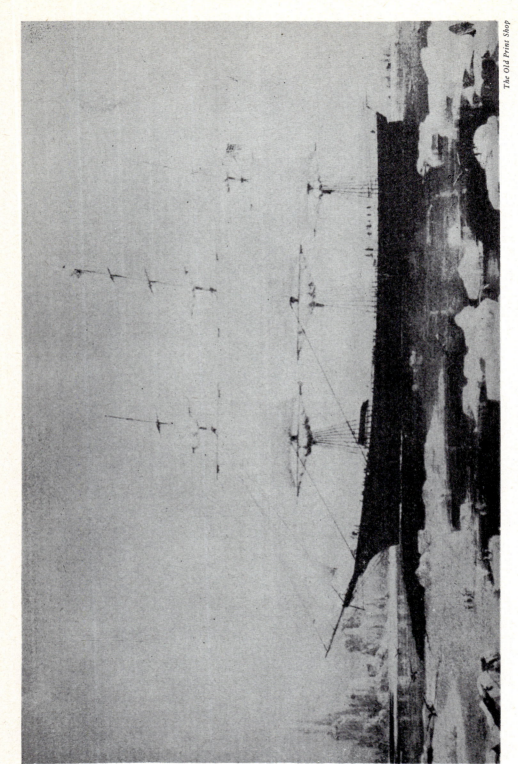

*(Illustration 98) Red Jacket, a Large-Folio Print.*

*(Illustration 99)* "The Road—Winter," by N. Currier, after original by Knirsch. In this large-folio print, Mr. and Mrs. Currier are shown in a cutter.

(*Illustration 100*)  **The Earliest Baseball Print, Published in 1862 by Currier & Ives.**

By 1723 he had his own shop and his name had been Anglicized as Paul Revere. In early eighteenth-century America, Boston was the center of colonial wealth with a growing demand for such household luxuries as silver plate which was both a symbol of gentle living and a good investment. The elder Paul prospered and made the name of Revere a synonym for fine silver. His son, Paul, the third of thirteen children, carried on the tradition and made it celebrated.

Most of the silver bearing the Revere mark still in existence was made by Paul the patriot and a man of many accomplishments. He was born in 1735 and was trained in his father's shop where his apprenticeship included designing and making various types of hollow ware as well as chasing and engraving. On the death of his father in 1754, Paul II, then nineteen years of age, inherited a well-established business.

The Georgian style was in favor at the time and he worked in that rococo fashion until the start of the American Revolution when the numerous patriotic demands on his time and energy interfered seriously with the silversmithing business. After the war, he worked in the classic style, which had been introduced in England by the Brothers Adam, and produced some of his finest pieces during the closing years of the eighteenth century. The fluted sugar urn in Illustration 88 is a typical example. The steepled cover has a scalloped rim and is surmounted by a cone-shaped finial. The body is of classic outline with fluting and bright-cut ornamentation. This piece has an auction record price of $2,200. Artistically it compares favorably with the best work of such English silversmiths as Hester Bateman (Illustration 93).

Paul Revere lived to be eighty-three years old and was apparently successful in whatever he undertook, whether in craftsmanship, business, or civic affairs. Besides his fine hollow ware, he also devoted himself to spoon-making, the backbone of silversmithing business in America. Many families who could not afford fine table pieces were good customers for spoons of varying sizes. In Illustration 89 there are two views of a Paul Revere teaspoon. A chased design, bright-cut with the initials of owner, ornaments the front of the handle. The upper view is of the back of spoon and shows his touch mark, "REVERE" in an oblong, on the center of handle.

During his long life he used five touch marks. The earliest, "P. REVERE" in rectangle, was probably the one used by his father. Then came "REVERE" in rectangle with pellet before; "PR" in capital script in rectangle, either alone or with second mark; REVERE in rectangle, and the same with lower left corner cut.

### What Is Sheffield Plate?

There are two satisfactory substitutes for solid silver—Sheffield plate and electroplate. The first was made in Sheffield, England, from about 1750 on; the other a full century later. The eighteenth-century plated ware came into being by accident when Thomas Boulsover of Sheffield in mending a broken knife handle unintentionally fused silver and copper.

He made a few small experimental pieces in this new material. One of his apprentices, Josiah Hancock, carrying on the process, began to make artistic pieces and an important industry was started. Factories for its making were established not only in Sheffield but in Birmingham, London, and on the Continent.

In preparing Sheffield plate, a block of copper was cleaned and smoothed, a thin plate of silver laid over it, the two wired together and placed in a charcoal furnace until the silver began to melt. Upon removal, the piece was treated like silver. Further experiments during the second half of the eighteenth century resulted in a silver coating on both sides, thus forming a metal sandwich with copper for the filling.

Style and workmanship closely followed that of solid silver. The labor involved in preparing Sheffield plate and making it into various pieces was undoubtedly greater than in regular silversmithing, but the cost of materials was so much less that the buyer of moderate means could have a fine pair of candlesticks for half the price of silver ones of the same design and size. He would also save the heavy government tax then levied on solid silver. This last factor appealed also to those who could afford the more costly ware.

The examples in Illustration 90 are typical of the handsome articles made in Sheffield plate. In the center is a large platter with domed cover engraved with a coat of arms. The platter is removable and rests on a shallow hot-water compartment with small button feet and handles matching that of the cover. Made about 1830, all parts bear the mark of J. Watson & Son. The pair of four-light Georgian candlesticks bear the name-mark Dever, a maker of Sheffield plate, *circa* 1790-1800, whose identity has not yet been established. The candlesticks have removable branching arms, thus making the sticks adaptable for either one or four-light use.

Sheffield was popular from 1750 to 1840 when the still cheaper process of electroplating succeeded it. Old Sheffield can be distinguished from solid silver by the undersides of its edges. To hide the reddish copper line between the two silver layers, the upper one was either drawn over the copper or a covering border of silver was applied. This resulted in a fine line which can be either felt or seen. This also distinguishes it from modern electroplate. Further, the basic material of the latter is a soft alloy, not unlike pewter, known as white metal. It has a disconcerting lack of resistance to heat, as anyone who has accidentally set a electroplated teapot or platter too close to the heat can testify.

Sheffield plate, on the other hand, could take such punishment. In two enemies are time and usage. These eventually wear away the silver coating and show the copper base beneath.

### Electroplated Silver, Successor to Pewter

Pewter was the poor man's silver in America from the mid-seventeenth century to about 1850. During these two hundred years, workers in this perishable alloy were, like the silversmiths, craftsmen who served lengthy apprenticeships and then worked at their trade, producing articles and shapes akin to those of silver but simpler and plainer in decorative detail.

Then, by the second decade of the nineteenth century, the inexpensive and colorful earthenware dishes from Staffordshire and tableware of silver

82

fused on copper from Sheffield began giving them keen competition. Consequently, when an electrolytic process for silver plating was discovered and perfected in England, American pewterers were quick to capitalize on it. The new method presented few problems to them as the soft white alloy under the silver was so similar to pewter that it could be worked with the same tools and spinning methods; furthermore, it did not call for such a high percentage of tin, the most expensive component of pewter.

The man who laid the foundation for this important nineteenth-century American industry was John O. Mead, a Philadelphia pewterer who went to England, learned the silver-plating technique in Birmingham, and then returned to experiment further. In 1845, he and William Rogers of Hartford, Connecticut, became partners and began making electroplated flatware. It was a commercial success, although the partnership lasted only a year. Mead returned to Philadelphia and resumed his own silver-plating business there. Rogers stayed in Hartford and, with his brothers, Asa and Simeon, formed the famous company, trademarked "Rogers Brothers, 1847."

By the 1850's, a number of pewter craftsmen had shifted their operations to the manufacturing of silver-plated wares in various forms, ranging from tea and coffee services to butter dishes, casters, cake dishes, platters, tureens, and other table ware. Among the large manufacturers besides Rogers Brothers, were Reed and Barton of Taunton, Massachusetts, who began electroplating in 1848, and the Meriden Britannia Company, founded in 1852 in Meriden, Connecticut, and by 1863 the largest maker of plated silver in America.

Since this change from pewter to electroplated silver occurred at the height of the Victorian period, the pieces made in the new ware are always more elaborate in design than the earlier pewter, which was generally very plain and simple. Not only are the silver-plated pieces ornamented with Victorian details but they are often embellished with florid engraved decoration.

A sure way to distinguish pewter from its successor is by the maker's mark. The pewter's mark is stamped into the piece with a steel die; the silver plater's is frequently a small coin-like disk, soldered to the bottom of a piece, with the letters raised, as shown in the insert in Illustration 91. Many of these marks are the names of companies with their place-names and also include the word "quadruple" or "quadruple plate" to indicate quality of plating. A pewter touch mark is generally either a name or initials, plain or combined with some decorative design such as an eagle, rose and crown, or similar device.

The silver-plated service in the illustration is in the Victorian manner but of restrained classic outline. It is decorated with beading and bands of Greek-key pattern. Originally, it included two pots, one for tea and a larger one for coffee. The maker's label is on the bottom of each piece, a coin-like disk lettered, "Rogers, Smith & Co., New Haven Ct." with "No. 1790" in the center. This was one of William Rogers numerous partnerships. The figure, 1790, is the style number and not the year the service was made. The approximate date can be established as after 1862 and before 1868, since the Rogers, Smith factory was moved from Hartford to New Haven in 1862 and six years later to Meriden.

There were capable silversmiths in America from the middle of the seventeenth century. The earliest of them naturally had to combine their calling with one or more other trades to make a living in a land so newly settled but, by the beginning of the eighteenth century, many of the 200,000 Americans living along the Atlantic seaboard were prosperous enough to afford some silver in their homes.

The majority of them, especially in New England, Pennsylvania, and New York, patronized native silversmiths. However, there was a more or less steady flow of imported silver from the mother country. In Virginia and the Carolinas especially, plantation owners were the chief purchasers of such luxuries as china, textiles, and silver. According to old records, many of them kept funds in London and commissioned their factors there to send them clothing and household goods "in the newest and latest fashion."

George Washington, being a Virginian, followed this custom. Among the New England families who bought English silver during the eighteenth century was that of Tobias Lear, private secretary and close friend of Washington. At least a dozen pieces are still in existence today.

At the beginning of the eighteenth century, the beautiful Queen Anne silver had little or no decoration. Later, the florid ornamentation of the rococo style held the public taste from about 1735 to 1770. But toward the close of the century there was a return to simplicity, the classic style of the Adam period dominating silver design. Bright-cut engraving was a favorite method of ornamentation.

Silver of the Queen Anne period or early eighteenth century undoubtedly appealed to the plain tastes of the American colonist. The design of the candlesticks in Illustration 92, which were made in London in 1716, continued in favor for over a century. The octagonal base and pear-shaped stem and the cylindrical candleholder were a combination both practical and pleasing to the eye.

The lighthouse coffee pot, so-called because of its form, was made in London in 1721 by Paul Lamerie. Considered the greatest of English silversmiths, he was born in Holland in 1688 where his Huguenot parents had fled from religious persecution in France. They later settled in England where Paul became a London silversmith, working there from 1710 to the end of his life in 1751. His name is practically synonymous with the rococo style, but he was equally expert with the unornamented Queen Anne style as is apparent from this example. Save for floral engraving on the spout, this coffee pot depends for its beauty on proportion.

In addition to the regular hallmarks, English silversmiths used individual touch marks which were duly registered. Lamerie had four. The first had the letters "LA" with crown and star above and cross below; the second, "PL" with pellet between, crown and lozenge above, and cross below, registered in 1724, appears on this piece made in 1729. The position of its ear-shaped wooden handle is unusual.

Up to fifty years ago, England was a man's world. Women had few rights that husbands and male relatives could not invade. Only a Queen, like Elizabeth I, occupying the throne in her own right, was free of this masculine domination. Otherwise, law and custom gave men control of all property and rendered them superior beings to be obeyed without question by their women folk.

Such was the law. In actual practice, however, from the fifteenth century on, England had her share of forceful women who conducted business in their own names on an equal footing with men. Nowhere was this more evident than with silversmiths. Those doing business in London had to be members of the Worshipful Company of Goldsmiths and record their maker's marks at Goldsmith's Hall. This record of touch marks with the names of the craftsmen who had entered them dates back to 1697.

During the century and a half that followed, there were sixty-three women members of the Goldsmiths Company, each with her own distinctive touch mark which was always part of the series called hallmarks. These identify a piece of London silver, even to the year it was made. They are: crowned leopard's head, signifying "made in London," the date-letter, year of making; lion passant, fineness of metal; sovereign's head, luxury tax paid; and individual craftsman's touch, usually one or two initials.

Among the women silversmiths, Hester Bateman is pre-eminent, possibly because she raised three sons and a daughter who all followed the craft or because her silver was as nicely executed as any by her male competitors. At any rate, pieces of Bateman silver have long been owned in America and are of partiular interest to collectors now.

There is no record of where she was born or under whom she served her apprenticeship. From 1774 to about 1825, the Bateman shop was located on Bunhill Road. Here, in 1790, she was joined in the craft by her sons, Peter, Jonathan, and William, and by her daughter, Ann. Hester's first mark, entered in 1774, was the script letters "HB" in an scalloped oval. In 1790, Peter and Jonathan entered their mark, a square with initials "PB" above "I.B." In 1795, another square mark, "PB" above "AB," was entered for Peter and Ann. Finally, in 1800, the last Bateman mark, an oblong with initials "PB, AB and WB," one over the other. This was used by Peter, Ann, and William when they formed their silversmithing partnership. Their mother, by that time had either died or retired, but for a quarter of a century, together or separately, the three continued as active London silversmiths.

Although the silver designs used by the Bateman family varied somewhat during a span of fifty years, most of it was of classic lines and often ornamented with bright-cut engraving. Fine examples of the Adam influence are seen in Illustration 93. The silver teapot at the left was made in 1783. It has an indistinct mark but probably was the work of Hester. The sugar bowl at right was made by her son Peter and daughter Ann in 1817 and, like the teapot, is decorated with bright-cut engraving.

# V

# Prints

### A Currier & Ives Masterpiece

FROM THE BEGINNING to the end of its long publishing career, the firm of Currier & Ives was keenly aware of what the public wanted. In 1861, when the Civil War had taken so many men from the farms to the battlefields, they published a number of peaceful genre prints which had great appeal as an escape from the prevailing war hysteria. One of the best of these is the colorful "Husking" (Illustration 94).

The original of this print was painted by Eastman Johnson about 1860. Although painted in New York, the scene could well have been somewhere in Maine where the artist was born and where he spent the first twenty years of his life. A successful painter for some sixty years, he was born in 1824 and died in 1906, his years of artistic productivity coinciding with the heyday of the lithographic print. Although he is known primarily as a portrait painter, his preference was for genre painting, and it is now generally agreed that it was unfortunate that he did not devote himself more to this field. The color and brilliance of his large canvas, "Cornhusking," is excellently reproduced in the Currier & Ives print. Indeed, many European art experts consider it the finest lithograph ever done in America. The only painting of Johnson's issued by Currier & Ives, it was published in the large folio, drawn on stone by the lithographer Severin, and hand-colored by an unknown artist. These water-colorists, for the most part anonymous, worked on the large-folio prints at the rate of one dollar per dozen and the excellence of their work accounts for much of the fine quality of Currier & Ives prints.

In this autumn scene, the light of the late afternoon sun picks up the bright yellow of the cornstalks on the barn floor and sharply outlines the figures. At the left is an old man braiding a cluster of orange-colored ears to be used as seed for another year. In the center, the farmer carries a basketful of husked ears on his shoulder. At the right is a young woman whose work has been interrupted by a neighbor who has dropped in with his dog and a brace of ducks, the latter possibly to be roasted for the supper which followed a husking and made of it a social occasion.

The original painting from which this print was reproduced is in the collection of The Syracuse Museum of Fine Arts. The colors have dimmed somewhat with the passing of the years so that the light of the afternoon sun and the other highlights are now shown to better advantage in a good copy of the print.

### Durrie and The New England Farm

The scenes of childhood have always had a nostalgic appeal whether celebrated in song or shown on canvas. During the nineteenth century, prosperous settlers of the Middle West were prone to view the eastern country scene through a rosy mist of memory. Paintings and lithographs of the period usually depict a farm scene with rolling hills in the background and a friendly little house, a brook, a dog, and various signs of rural life in the foreground.

Among the artists who portrayed the country scene, George H. Durrie painted unusually realistic pictures of the farm as home and center of happy family life. So warm and human was his treatment of his subject that his canvases had great appeal and lithographs produced from them sold widely. Currier & Ives brought out ten. One is an autumn scene of cidermaking and nine are winter scenes. The most famous is the rare and valuable "Home to Thanksgiving" (Illustration 95). Four other Durrie paintings were reproduced as prints by other American lithographers.

George H. Durrie was born in New Haven, Connecticut, in 1820. His father, John Durrie, was a book publisher and his mother, Clarissa Clark, was a descendant of William Bradford of the Massachusetts Bay Colony. He spent his boyhood in New Haven, opened a studio there in 1841 and the same year married Susan Perkins. He began his career as a portrait painter and lived for a while in Freehold, New Jersey, then briefly in Petersburg, Virginia. But the New England scene soon drew him back to New Haven. There he spent the rest of his life and turned from portrait painting to the rural scenes which found such favor during his lifetime and are appreciated so keenly today.

His life in New Haven was apparently as placid and happy as the scenes which he painted. He prospered and built a large house on Temple Street which included a big room for use as a studio. He found plenty of subjects for his canvases in the countryside around New Haven, notably in Cheshire, the town just north of New Haven, where farm buildings and general scenes have changed but little.

Durrie painted what he had been familiar with all his life. The result is at the same time realistic and romantic. The farm buildings, animals, and people are all there but as types instead of actual portraits. Consequently, a transplanted New Englander who had started life on a farm could see in one of Durrie's paintings the reflection of his own boyhood in the mellow light of memory.

"Home to Thanksgiving" was painted in 1861, only two years before

Durrie's death. Currier & Ives published the large-folio print from it in 1867, two years after the close of the Civil War when such subjects as home and family reunions appealed strongly to the public. Lithographs of this and of other good paintings then sold for a dollar and a half to three dollars. Today this particular print is valued at a price that would astonish those purveyors of moderately-priced works of art to the American people. The large-folio prints measure about eighteen by twenty-seven inches, and to be of prime value now should be in good condition, clear, unstained, and with margins uncut.

All of the Currier & Ives prints of winter scenes reproduced from Durrie paintings are valuable and in demand. Among those of special interest, besides "Home to Thanksgiving," are two companion prints "Winter in the Country —The Old Grist Mill" and "Winter in the Country—Getting Ice," this last possibly the scarcest of all the winter scenes, and "New England Winter Scene" (Illustration 96), which, though not the rarest, is one of the most pleasing. Painted in 1860 and published in 1861 by Currier & Ives, it shows a Connecticut farmhouse with barn and other outbuildings in the background. The farm animals and fowls are shown in natural poses. There are various household and farm items scattered about, showing that not even in that leisurely time did everything get put away in its proper place.

Such realistic pictures of happy family life in the country, done with almost photographic attention to detail, probably accounts for the renewed appreciation of those Durrie paintings that were never reproduced as lithographs. These paintings now bring ten times the price at which they could have been bought only a few years ago.

### Clipper-Ship Prints

The picture that started Nathaniel Currier on his career of publishing colored prints was of a ship—"The Awful Conflagration of the Steam Boat *Lexington*." This occurred, January 13, 1840, on Long Island Sound and Currier lithographed it as a half-page illustration for the *New York Sun*. It was followed by more than three hundred other prints of all kinds of vessels —clippers, steamships, and river craft. Those of the fast clipper ships form a distinct group.

The era of these sailing ships began just before 1845 and closed about twenty years later with the opening of the Suez Canal. These clippers specialized in the China tea trade, were active during the California gold rush, and engaged in the long run to Australia. They carried both passengers and cargoes and established many speed records, such as twelve days from Boston to Liverpool, less than ninety days from New York to San Francisco, eighty-one days from Calcutta to New York, and around the world in 134 days. All clippers were specially designed for fast sailing. They were built with sharply curved bow, unusual depth of keel, and tapering hull. Their towering three or four masts carried so much sail that large crews were needed to handle them. They averaged 1500 to 2500 tons burden and in many instances were beautifully fitted. Donald McKay of Boston was the foremost builder of clipper ships. The record voyages were so much talked about that there was a great demand for pictures of these speed queens. Currier was always ready to fill such a demand and in 1845 published his first clipper-ship print, "Outward Bound." In 1849 he issued a pair, "The Gem of the Atlantic" and "The Gem of the Pacific."

These were followed by nearly twenty more, of which "The American Clipper Ship, *Witch of the Waves*" (Illustration 97) is held to be the best of the small-folio clipper prints. It is undated but was issued by N. Currier about 1852. This clipper was built in 1851 by George Raynes at Portsmouth, New Hampshire, for the California gold trade. One of the most beautiful clippers ever launched, she was a very speedy ship and made many record voyages. Most of these small-folio clipper prints are undated. About half of them appeared after 1857 with the Currier & Ives imprint.

The majority of these later prints are not pictures of specific ships but dramatic views with such titles as "A Clipper Ship in a Snow Squall," "A Squall off Cape Horn," "Off a Lee Shore," "Off the Coast in a Snow Storm—Taking a Pilot," "A Clipper in a Hurricane—*The Comet* off Bermuda" and "An American Clipper Ship Off Sandy Hook in a Snow Storm." Last of this group, issued much later in 1870, was "Clipper Ship *The Three Brothers*."

There are but fifteen early clipper-ship prints in the large-folio size. With one exception, they were published between 1851 and 1854 by the enterprising Nathaniel Currier. They all bear the year issued and the imprint, "N. Currier." The sole exception is the "Clipper Ship *Challenge*" which was the work of Endicott, another prolific producer of lithographic prints. All fifteen show the ships under sail, such as the print entitled "Clipper Ship *Red Jacket*—In the Ice off Cape Horn on Her Passage from Australia to Liverpool, August 1854" (Illustration 98).

In addition, there are two later prints published by Currier & Ives, which also record the brief span when these sailing ships were the speed queens of the Atlantic and Pacific. They are "Clipper Ship *Three Brothers*" issued in 1875 and "Clipper Ship *Flying Cloud*," done in 1880 as a reissue of the same subject originally published by N. Currier.

The early prints portray twelve different American ships. In the order of publication they are of the clippers, *Dreadnaught, Sovereign of the Seas, Racer, Hurricane, Flying Cloud, Young America, Sweepstakes, Comet, Great Republic* (three slightly different views of the ship as completed and as rebuilt after being burned), *Nightingale, Red Jacket,* a second *Dreadnaught* (shown off Fushar Light) and *Challenge* (done by Endicott).

Usually Currier published his large-folio clipper prints upon the launching of the ships or shortly after they had made record voyages. This was the case with the *Red Jacket* print, now considered one of the most pleasing of this group. Copies in mint condition have sold at auction for $1,250. This clipper ship was built at Rockland, Maine. Her maiden voyage in February, 1854, was from New York to Liverpool, done in thirteen days and one hour, despite continuous rain, snow, or hail all the way. That same year, under English charter, she entered the Australian trade and established more records. The one from Liverpool to Melbourne was made in sixty-nine days. On the return, carrying 45,000 ounces of gold, she reached Liverpool in seventy-three days, in spite of considerable time lost off Cape Horn because of field-ice and icebergs as shown in the illustration.

The *Red Jacket's* figurehead was a full-length carving of the famous Indian chief for whom she was named. She registered 2,006 tons, was 260 feet long, had a 44-foot beam and a draft of 26 feet. After her first round trip to Australia, she was sold to Pilkington & Wilson for £30,000. They continued her in the Australian trade for several years during which she became one of the most famous of the American-built clippers. She ended her days in the Quebec lumber trade.

This *Red Jacket* print was done on stone by Charles Parsons, one of the foremost of these marine artists, who worked first for N. Currier and later for Currier & Ives. Parsons' name is to be found on nine other clipper-ship prints.

Any large-folio print of an American clipper ship is desirable. Shown under sail with beauty and fidelity, they have long been popular with collectors, and consequently, are now scarce and bring very high prices.

### Winter Sports

Back in the nineteenth century when northern snows came early and stayed late, when Whittier glorified the delights of the New England winter in "Snow-bound," when there were no automobiles and consequently no highways to be kept open, deep snows were accepted as a proper part of winter.

Wheeled vehicles were put away. Sleighs and sleds were brought out. Sleigh bells jingled and traffic moved by living, breathing horse power. A pair of fast horses harnessed to a cutter got over the ground with a speed and smoothness not equalled at any other time of the year. Other winter pastimes were skating, coasting, ice boating, fishing through the ice, hunting, and, toward spring, the rural social event known as a "sugaring off party." All these are depicted in the numerous prints issued by Currier & Ives.

Probably the sport which appealed to all ages because it was also a means of transportation was sleighing. The large-folio print in Illustration 99 is typical. Entitled "The Road, Winter," it was published by N. Currier in 1853, a few years before the famous partnership was formed. The scene was drawn by Otto Knirsch who worked for Currier for some years and later went into business for himself as a lithographer.

The country landscape with the light of late afternoon on it forms a background for the span of horses drawing a cutter in which a man and woman are seated amid fur robes. They are Nathaniel Currier and his wife, Lura Ormsbee. The staff of his printing establishment produced this as a Christmas present for their employer. He liked it so much that he added it to the general list. It is now an expensive rarity.

Besides this placid sleighing scene, N. Currier and Currier & Ives published some five different prints bearing the title of "The Sleigh Race." The scarcest is a small folio showing two one-horse sleighs speeding along side by side with one horse a little more than a half-head in advance. Each sleigh is occupied by a man and woman dressed in the costume of the day.

Another small-folio print, entitled "Central Park in Winter," shows a number of cutters in the foreground of all sorts, from large ones drawn by four horses to spans and singles. In the background is the skating pond crowded with skaters. This was published after James Ives became Currier's partner.

Sleighing was a favorite pastime for both men and the drive along the skating pond in Central Park must have been familiar to them.

Skating parties were popular in both city and country during the Victorian years. Another scene, drawn by Charles Parsons, shows the skating pond in Central Park, where hoop-skirted women attended by silk-hatted men are skimming over the ice. It was published in large folio by Currier & Ives in 1862 under the title "Central Park, Winter—The Skating Pond."

### Baseball Prints

Baseball is now over a hundred and fifteen years old. Its birthplace was Cooperstown, New York, and it was evolved from a now forgotten game called "town ball" by one Abner Doubleday, a student at a military school there. Abner could not have foreseen the far reaching results of what he started with a ball, bat, and nine boys in 1839, when sports were mainly confined to horse racing, boat racing, and county-fair wrestling matches.

Baseball remained an amateur game until the latter part of the nineteenth century and the prints depicting various games were few in number. During the 1860's there were a few pieces of sheet music published, such as "The Home Run Polka," which bear on their covers a lithograph of some phase of the game. There is also a print showing a Confederate military prison with a baseball game taking place within the stockade. This is called "Union Prisoners at Salisbury, N. C.," and was published by Sarony, Major, and Knapp, New York lithographers and competitors of Currier & Ives. Its sub-title states that it was "drawn from nature by Act. Major Otto Boetticher." He may or may not have been one of the prisoners, but the emphasis with this print is more on the prison than on the game.

Probably the most important print with baseball as the subject is the large folio entitled "The American National Game of Baseball. Grand Match for the Championship at the Elysian Fields, Hoboken, N. J." (Illustration 100). Published in 1862 by Currier & Ives, it was drawn by an unknown artist. Whoever he was, his work is far above the average as to action and setting. This rare and important print is illustrated in color in *Currier & Ives, Printmakers to the American People*, by the well-known authority, the late Harry T. Peters. He considered the print one of the finest ever published by this firm.

Aside from its artistic merit, baseball fans will find it interesting as showing a time when the game was still very young. Grandstands and stadiums were still in the future. Players' uniforms are informal and the spectators stand around in groups or sit in their carriages. Silk-hatted gentlemen brush elbows with those in less formal attire and it is doubtful if anyone raised the cry of "Kill the Umpire!" Incidentally, the umpire is dressed in a Prince Albert coat and a pork-pie hat.

This appears to be the only large-folio baseball print published by Currier & Ives. They were true prophets regarding the importance of the national game, since the big leagues had come into existence before they finally closed their doors. They used the game as a subject five times in their comic prints. It is an interesting fact, however, that no artist seems to have used the game as a subject for a formal oil painting.

91

Voting for a candidate on Election Day a hundred years ago was no private matter. Although printed lists had superseded the earlier practice of verbal voting in practically all of the thirty-one states, proceedings at the polls were still informal and uninhibited. There were few state regulations, no voting booths, no numbered ballots, and no ban on electioneering at the polling place. Ballots, usually of a distinctive color, were furnished by political organizations and distributed by party workers. Each voter, vigilantly watched by his party captain, presented his ballot to the moderator in full view of those present, and how he voted was no secret.

The print called "County Election" (Illustration 101) portrays a typical scene in Missouri during the 1850's. Drawn after a painting done in 1851 by George Caleb Bingham, it is one of four showing different campaign phases as he saw them, probably during his own campaign and election to the Missouri State legislature in 1848. The first two, "Canvassing for a Vote" and "County Election," were done in 1851; "Stump Speaking" and "The Verdict of the People," were done in 1854. Prints of all except the last were published and examples are still in existence. "County Election" was engraved by John Sartain in 1854 and published by Goupil et Cie, Paris. It measures 22⅛ by 30⅛ inches and is hand-colored. It may also be found in black and white.

The original painting of "Canvassing for a Vote" is now lost but prints of it, drawn by Regnier and published by Goupil in 1853, still exists. "Stump Speaking" was drawn by Gautier, originally published by Goupil and later by Fishel, Afler, and Schwartz, New York. It is the same size as the engraving of "County Election." "The Verdict of The People" was to have been published as a lithograph about 1870 but the stone on which it was drawn unfortunately was broken.

The artist who put the story of early political campaigns on canvas, George Caleb Bingham, was born in Virginia in 1811 and was taken by his family to Missouri when he was eight. There he spent the rest of his life save for a few years in Philadelphia and Europe where he studied art. He died in Kansas City in 1879 after a successful career of over forty years as a painter of genre subjects and portraits. He evidently took a keen interest in public affairs and the life about him. This is apparent especially in his genre paintings, which include, besides those already mentioned from which prints were made, "The Jolly Flatboatmen," published 1848, "In a Quandary," published 1852, and "The Emigration of Daniel Boone with His Family," published in 1852.

During his lifetime, his chief income was from his portraits. He is best appreciated today for his genre paintings, possibly because they were done during the years of his best work, from 1837 to 1856. In these paintings, both his skill as a portrait painter and his interest in humanity are strikingly exemplified.

### American Steel Engravings

Although many of us can remember seeing such steel engravings as "Washington and His Generals," "First Blow for Liberty," and similar historic subjects in the homes of our grandparents, these are among the heirlooms so far passed over by most collectors in favor of the colored prints by Currier & Ives and other lithographers. Yet they date from the same period.

Steel engravings were made from about 1835 to 1880. Those of small size were used mostly as book illustrations .The large folio were for framing. Some were hand-colored but the majority were published in black and white. Originally they were considerably more expensive than lithographs, but today they lag far behind. From five to about twenty-five dollars is a fair price for the black and white and possibly more than fifty dollars for the colored. Many of them can still be found in their original gold leaf frames.

In their way, they give just as interesting account of the American scene as the more costly lithographs but lack of demand keeps them in a low price group. It seems to me here is a chance for someone to assemble a good representative collection of these steel engravings. There is the excellent genre print, "County Elections" after Bingham's painting (Illustration 101), engraved by John Sartain of Philadelphia, one of the best and most prolific of American steel engravers. Another fine print is "Mexican News," engraved by Alfred Jones from the painting by R. C. Woodville.

Typical of American subjects done as steel engravings during the years of their popularity is "Washington and His Generals" (Illustration 102). It was drawn, engraved, and published by A. H. Ritchie in 1856 and was reissued in 1870 by Emil Seitz of New York. Ritchie was a Scotch painter who turned engraver after he came to the United States in 1841. He established an extensive business in New York where he continued for many years. Among his other engravings are "Lady Washington's Reception," after the painting by Daniel Huntington, and "The Emancipation Proclamation," from Carpenter's painting, which shows Lincoln reading that document to members of his cabinet.

Other good engravings are "Raising the Liberty Pole" and "Pulling Down the Statue of George III" by J. C. McRea. He is also known for a portrait of General Robert E. Lee. Scenic subjects are desirable, especially views of New York, Boston, and other cities, in large size, done by Mottram from drawings by J. W. Hill. Of little or no demand at present are sentimental subjects, such as "Deathbed of Daniel Webster," "Washington Irving and Friends," and others of such type.

### Kitten Prints

Although colored lithographs of playful kittens, published by Currier & Ives and their contemporaries, have been pretty much ignored by those who write about nineteenth-century prints, there is a sizeable group of people who prize them.

The majority of these kitten prints are small folio but there are some of medium size and one or two in the large folio. There are at least four reasons why people buy these prints: they like cats; they think the prints are nice for children's rooms; they consider them colorful and pleasing decorations in themselves; and lastly, they find in them nostalgic appeal—"just like a print in grandmother's house." These prints are relatively inexpensive. Most of them can be acquired, unframed, for less than twenty-five dollars. The few rarities can run as high as one hundred dollars.

Most kitten prints are either sentimental or playful. A few, like "Good Old Rover and Kittie" or "Good Fido and Naughty Kitty," combine dogs and cats. One, entitled "The Playmates," shows three girls, a canary, and a kitten. Another, "The Cats-Paw," shows a cat, kitten, and a monkey. The majority depict the cat alone, preferably in the kitten stage and in action.

Today the three prints most often seen and most popular are: "My Little White Kitties Learning Their ABC" (playing with alphabet blocks); "My Little White Kitties Playing Dominoes"; and "My Little White Kitties Playing Ball," the last dated 1870, which is unusual. Most of the kitten prints are undated. These "White Kittie" prints were published by Currier & Ives who produced over fifty kitten and cat prints during their long career. One of the rarest, entitled "Kitty" and bearing the imprint of N. Currier, is a vignette of a gray kitten with a doll in a basket in the background. It was probably published shortly before the name of the firm was changed in 1857 to Currier & Ives. Kitten prints seldom bear the name of the artist. One exception is a large folio entitled "Kitty's Breakfast" signed by L. Maurer, another Currier & Ives artist especially known for his horse prints.

This firm and other American lithographers adapted many of their kitten prints from those of European origin, especially of English and German provenance. "The Playful Family" (Illustration 103) was published by the Kelloggs of Hartford, Connecticut, from a European original. It is undated, as is a later one with the same title and similar poses published by Currier & Ives.

The Hartford firm was composed of three brothers—Daniel, Edmund B., and Elijah C. Kellogg. Daniel first worked alone from 1833 to 1842 and, in 1843, was joined by his two brothers. Until 1852 their imprint was "E. B. & E. C. Kellogg, 136 Main St., Hartford, Conn." They also had two branch offices, named at the left and right of the print illustrated: "Kellogg & Thayer, 144 Fulton St., N. Y." and "D. Needham, 223 Main St., Buffalo." Their prints, mostly in the small folio, had a wide sale, the volume even approaching that of Currier & Ives.

# VI

# Paintings

### Portraits of George Washington

"**I** SIT LIKE PATIENCE on a monument whilst they are delineating the lines of my face. . . . At first I was as impatient at the request and as restive under the operation as a colt is of the saddle. The next time I submitted very reluctantly, but with less flouncing; now no dray moves more readily to the thill than I do to the painter's chair."

Thus wrote George Washington in 1785 of how accustomed he had become to posing for his portrait. It all started in 1772 when, to please his wife, he posed for Charles Willson Peale in his uniform as colonel in the Virginia militia. From then until 1798, when he sat for his last portrait hardly a year before his death, Washington posed for at least eighteen, and possibly twenty-one, artists. The results were forty-six or more portraits painted from life and about four hundred and fifty copies made by the same artists from their originals.

There was a great demand for Washington portraits. Cities and towns of the new nation, the colleges and universities, prominent people both in America and abroad—all wanted a portrait of the first president. The English peer, the Earl of Buchan, sent the Scotch artist, Archibald Robertson, to the United States especially for that purpose.

Best known of the artists who painted Washington from life were Gilbert Stuart, John Trumbull, Joseph Wright, Robert Edge Pina, and the four members of the talented Peale family—Charles Willson, James, Charles Polk, and Rembrandt Peale. All of these artists did two or more portraits at different dates and they were all inclined to idealize the sitter.

Washington's natural dignity and poise are of course apparent in all of the portraits. His fine points were emphasized and any physical blemishes

95

omitted. Gilbert Stuart's unfinished head, which is undoubtedly the best known Washington portrait, is acknowledged to be the most famous picture in American art. It has come to be accepted by the American people as the one and only authentic conception of the first President of the United States.

Of all the Washington portraits there is just one that approximates a photograph showing him as he actually appeared in the flesh (Illustration 104). This little-known canvas was painted for the Masonic Lodge at Alexandria, Virginia, of which Washington was charter Worshipful Master. It still hangs in the lodge rooms and is carefully preserved as are other Washington heirlooms there.

In 1793 the lodge requested the privilege of having a portrait painted. It was granted and William Williams, a native New York artist, was engaged to paint it and instructed to "paint him as he is." So, although the portrait is rather primitive, it is a treasure of great historical significance. The smallpox scars and the disfiguring mark on his left cheek where a wen had been removed by a surgeon's knife are all clearly delineated. There is a mole under his right ear. But even in this canvas the great and commanding personality of the man render mere surface blemishes unimportant.

### *Ralph Earl, Connecticut's First Great Painter*

From about 1790 to 1801 Ralph Earl was the favored portrait painter of Connecticut. Many of his paintings hang in our leading museums. Occasionally one unknown to art experts comes to light. Usually its owner knows little more about it than the name of his forebear who sat for the likeness. He has paid no attention to the artist's signature and date, which is usually on the back of the canvas, covered by the dust of years.

Such discoveries of works by Earl are possible because during this period the artist tramped from town to town doing portraits whenever he could find people willing to pay for them. He kept no list of his work, so left few clues for locating his pictures. Since art critics recognized him about 1920 as the first realist among our native American painters, his work is considered highly desirable.

Ralph Earl was born in 1751 at Shrewsbury, Massachusetts, fifth generation of a typical New England Puritan family. His first art teacher was Samuel King of Newport, Rhode Island. By 1774 Earl was earning his living in New Haven as a portrait painter. The next year, going with the Connecticut troops, he saw the fighting at Lexington and Concord. There he made eye-witness sketches of these clashes from which his companion, Amos Doolittle, also of New Haven, engraved his first American battle-scene prints. About 1779, Earl sailed to England, became a pupil of Benjamin West and, in 1784, was elected to the Royal Academy. Two years later he was back in America where he painted portraits in New York City, sometimes with his subjects coming to pose in the debtor's prison. In 1790, he moved to Connecticut where he worked as an itinerant painter until his death in 1801 at Bolton.

During those years, he did many portraits of fathers and young sons, mothers with babes in arms, so typical of his work, and of husbands and

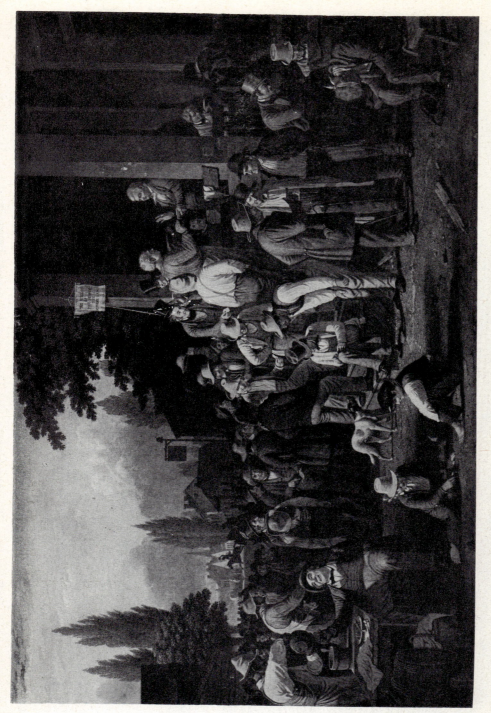

(*Illustration 101*) "County Election." Engraved by Sarrain after painting by Bingham.

(*Illustration 102*) "Washington and His Generals," a Steel Engraving by A. H. Ritchie.

(*Illustration 103*) "The Playful Family." Copied by Kellogg from a European print.

*(Illustration 104)* George Washington as a Mason, painted by William Williams. The only portrait showing Washington's facial blemishes.

*(Illustration 105)* "Oliver Ellsworth and His Wife," by Ralph Earl.

*(Illustration 106)* "Return from Market," by John Lewis Krimmel.

*Charles Zimmerman*

*(Illustration 107)* "Charles H. Brown," by Charles Loring Elliott.

*Arther Susel*

*(Illustration 108)* Typical Victorian Portrait of Children, artist unknown.

(*Illustration 109*) "Yankee Peddler," by John Whetton Ehninger.

*(Illustration 110)* "Trappers at Fault, Looking for the Trail," by Arthur Fitzwilliam Tait.

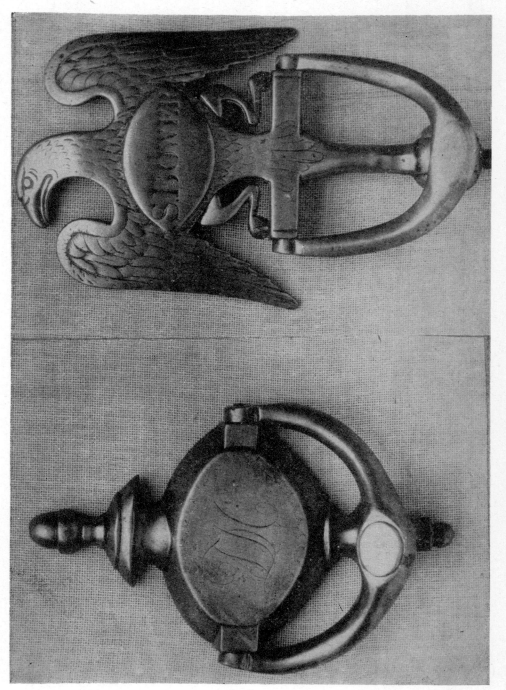

*(Illustration 111)* American Brass Door Knockers, ca. 1800-1825.

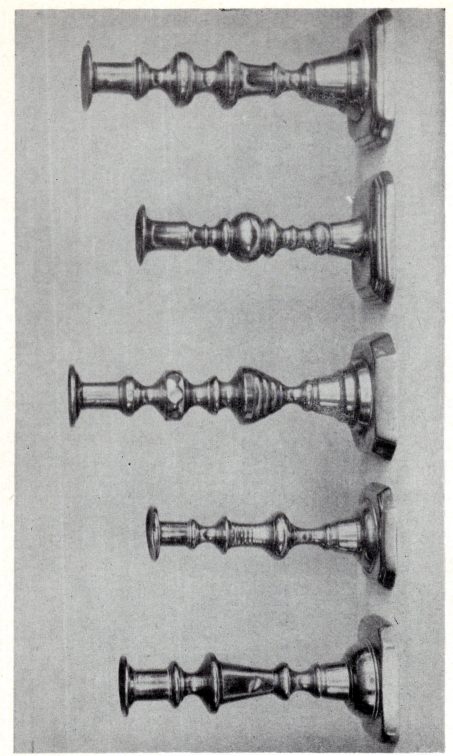

*(Illustration 112)* Five Typical Birmingham Brass Candlesticks, ca. 1800-1840.

(*Illustration 113*) Trotting Horse Weathervane, ca. 1870. Both man and horse are hollow, made of stamped sheet copper.

*(Illustration 114)* American Brass and Wrought Iron Andirons.

*(Illustration 115)* **Typical Sheet-Iron Lantern, American, ca. 1750-1825.**

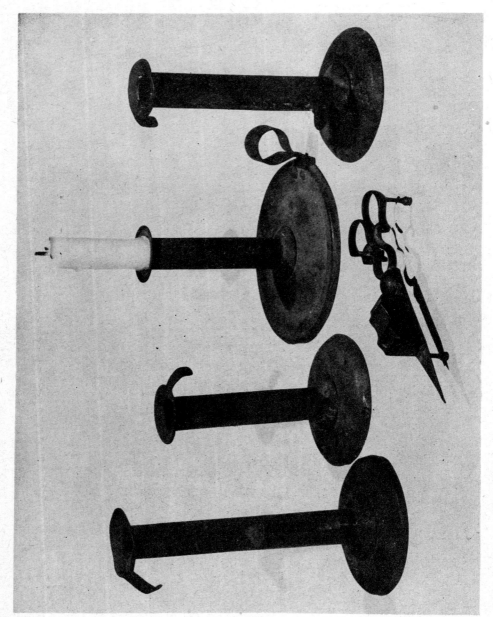

*(Illustration 116)* American Wrought-Iron Candlesticks, ca. 1790-1830.

wives like that of Chief Justice and Mrs. Oliver Ellsworth (Illustration 105). Painted in 1792, it shows them sitting in the library of their home at Windsor, Connecticut. In the background is a window through which is seen the Ellsworth house and lands. This was a frequent Earl touch. Details of dress and room are also typical.

### Krimmel, Early American Genre Artist

Called the Hogarth of America by his contemporaries, John Lewis Krimmel was born in Germany in 1789. He was twenty-one when he joined his brother George in America with the idea of following his bent as an artist. The elder brother considered this impractical and clapped him into a Philadelphia counting house.

John kept his irksome job a few months and then left it and his brother's house. He took lodgings and began painting portraits. The first was of his landlady and her family. It was so well done that other commissions soon followed. As he painted equally well on ivory, he was also popular as a miniaturist. After his marriage, he increased his income by becoming art teacher at a young lady's seminary. Meanwhile he found time to paint some of the genre subjects for which he is best remembered today.

One of them "The Fourth of July in Center Square, Philadelphia" is now owned by the Pennsylvania Academy of Fine Arts. It shows the lively action and vivid portraiture for which he became famous. This is also apparent in Illustration 106, "Return from Market." The present location of this painting is in doubt, but it was reproduced as a mezzotint by the engraver Sartain and published by W. H. Bidwell of New York about 1830 as a premium print for *The Eclectic Magazine*. It was originally done in black and white and its sub-title runs, "Home Scene—With Presents."

Krimmel went back to Germany in 1817 but, after a short stay, came back to the United States where he found *The Eclectic Magazine* wanted to use some of his genre subjects as illustrations.

Up to this time, buyers of paintings had regarded genre subjects scarcely worthwhile as works of art. In 1820, *The Eclectic Magazine* published an engraving of Krimmel's "Country Wedding" and the popularity of his genre subjects grew, especially those entitled "White's Great Cattle Show and Grand Procession of the Victuallers," and "Burning of Masonic Hall." Shortly afterward, he was given a commission to paint a historical canvas of "Penn's Treaty with the Indians." It was never finished. Krimmel was drowned in a mill pond near Germantown, Pennsylvania, while sketching for the painting, in 1821.

Had it not been for his untimely death, he would probably have been among the artists whose work N. Currier would have been eager to use. The founding of that famous lithographing business occurred only fourteen years later. Krimmel, for his part, was always interested in current events and personalities and was one of the few in his day to put them on canvas. Many of his early genres have not survived but are known from the engravings, principally made by his friend and patron, Alexander Lawson.

Most of these prints are in black and white, though some are found washed with watercolor. Because Krimmel's active artistic life was only a little over ten years, his paintings are few in number and even the prints after them are not plentiful. They are in demand because of the kindly humor and neat detail with which the artist painted them.

### *Charles Loring Elliott, Portrait Painter*

The outstanding portrait painter of the United States in the mid-nineteenth century was an entirely American artist. Although many of his contemporaries had studied abroad, Charles Loring Elliott never left his native land. At the height of his career, he was hailed as the successor to Gilbert Stuart. Today, an impressive number of his paintings hang in leading museums but, except for art specialists, his work is not as well known to the general public as it should be.

A prolific artist, he painted more than seven hundred portraits of prominent men and women of his time. One of his pictures is occasionally found in a country antique shop and is a real discovery. This happened with the unsigned oval portrait of the genial gentleman in Illustration 107. The artist's signature in the lower corner had evidently disappeared when the canvas was later remounted as an oval. So superior was it to the average Victorian portrait and inscribed on the back "Portrait of Charles H. Brown of Boston," it demanded attention.

Identifying the artist was quite simple. Several standard books on American art show a number of Elliott portraits with the same firm drawing, natural likeness, and clear colors, making it certain that this was by the same brush. One art critic has observed that "although Elliott is sometimes overlooked, he was one of the most brilliant analysts of character among American artists."

He was born in Scipio, near Auburn, New York, in 1812. As a small boy, he showed his artistic bent by drawing horses in motion. His father, an architect, gave him no encouragement and put him to work as a clerk in a Syracuse store when his school days were over. But by 1834 Charles was studying art in New York. His first teacher was John Trumbull, then an old man of eighty, who advised him to concentrate on architecture. He then studied briefly under John Quidor, did some book illustrations, and returned to central New York where he was an itinerant artist for ten years.

During that time, he continued studying. A portrait by Gilbert Stuart was his model and inspiration, and his self-training was so thorough that in 1845 he returned to New York City and opened a studio. His portrait of John Ericson, the inventor, won him high praise and, the next year, four other portraits in the National Academy exhibition established his reputation. Financiers, art patrons, and leading writers were all eager to sit for him. Among them was Matthew Vassar, Poughkeepsie brewer, later to found the college that bears his name. Another was Fletcher Harper, the publisher. His portrait was sent to the Paris International Exposition of 1855 as the best example of American portrait painting.

Until his death in 1868, Elliott had as many portrait commissions as he could undertake. Although Stuart had died before Elliott began his studies, the latter was essentially his pupil. Thus, he evolved his own style of painting affable portraits which were dominated by the artist's masterly insight into the character and personality of the sitter.

### Portraits of Early Americans

Previous to 1839 when the daguerreotype was perfected, pencil and brush were the only means of recording human likenesses. There were trained artists at home and abroad to depict the wealthy and politically important, of course, but were it not for the unknown itinerant painters of a century and a half ago, we should have very little idea of how the average American of that time looked.

These men with a talent for getting the human image down on wood, canvas, or paper, worked mostly in New England, New York, and Pennsylvania. Some of them had a little training, a very few had even studied abroad, but most of them were self-taught and relied on native ability and the knowledge they had been able to pick up as sign- or coach-painters to depict what they saw.

Their clients were prosperous farmers and substantial citizens of small towns. Like the country craftsmen who made furniture, silver, and pewter, their work varied according to their artistic skill. But, with even the crudest paintings, there was a realism that art critics have recently begun to appreciate.

Although artists with a craft rather than an academic background must have worked in America from the closing years of the seventeenth century on, most of the so-called primitive paintings found today were painted between 1790 and 1860. They were done in oils, watercolors, and pastels. Canvas, of course, was usual for oils, but wood and even upholsterer's ticking were sometimes used.

Like the photographer of the 1870's and later, the itinerant painter had a set way of posing his subjects, with certain stage props to indicate the profession or occupation of the sitter—binoculars for a sea captain, a book for a clergyman or a lawyer, a doll or other toy for a child, a flower or a book for a woman. Some of these wayfaring artists even prepared a number of canvases with scenic or plain background and with the body of the subject completed, save for the head. Then as summer weather made traveling about the countryside feasible, they set out to secure commissions from clients living in small towns and on farms.

In many cases, the itinerant painter was a guest in the house while he executed portraits of the family, severally or sometimes as a group. With the time-saving device of a prepared canvas, the sitter had only to pose long enough for the head to be added and possibly the stage prop that labeled or flattered him, as the case might be. Most of the portraits are unsigned but a few are, and tradition has supplied enough information regarding the identity of these artist-craftsmen for a good-sized list of them to be assembled.

The artist who painted the portrait of the two children in Illustration 108 is unknown, but he obviously was not without some training. The subjects were two brothers, children of a Boston family, and the date was about 1844. The older child is dressed in a fawn-colored suit with white waistcoat and ruffled white collar; the other, scarcely more than an infant, is wearing a white frock with oval neck trimmed with blue ribbons. The pose is characteristic of the period. A colorful note is struck by the scarlet shawl on which the children

99

are sitting and by the small scarlet volume which the younger brother holds on his knees.

## Paintings That Tell a Story

Life in America during the nineteenth century was dramatically portrayed by a number of artists who took homely, everyday scenes as subjects for their canvases. Known as "genre" paintings, they are now records of social and economic activities in the rural United States of a century ago. Some of these artists found various phases of the New England countryside appealing, some painted scenes laid in the mountains of the South, and still others showed Indian life on the plains of the Middle West.

One artist, John Whetton Ehninger, depicted a type of merchant known throughout the country for close to two centuries. He called his painting "Yankee Peddler" (Illustration 109) and in it recorded faithfully how these commercial knights of the road sold their wares, what the customers were like, and what sort of things were sold. These peddlers naturally got their name from the fact that most of them were enterprising young men from New England who scraped together a few dollars, invested them in the trade items from that locality, and then went on foot or by horse-drawn wagon to sell their wares in almost every part of the country.

Beginning in the eighteenth and continuing through the nineteenth century, they went up and down the land, dispensing needles and pins, combs, cheap jewelry, dress goods, pewter articles, tinware, and occasionally the newest in household articles, such as pattern-glass tableware and novelties, along with gossip and news. The last two made any peddler a welcome visitor in remote villages and isolated farms. As his wares consisted of practically everything for which there was a demand, many of today's heirlooms were originally distributed in this manner.

Peddlers successful enough to afford a pair of horses and a covered wagon carried a fairly large stock of merchandise that often included silver teaspoons, shelf clocks, and similar household accessories. A peddler of this type, selling his wares on the village green of a rural town, was the subject of this example of genre art in the illustration. The artist, John Whetton Ehninger, a member of the Astor family, was born in 1827 in New York City. He graduated from Columbia College when he was twenty and then went to Europe to study art. This picture, done while abroad, was exhibited in 1854 at the National Academy of Design, New York.

In the course of a long and active career, he painted a number of genre subjects that vividly depict life in the United States at that time. In "The Yankee Peddler" one can almost see sales resistance crumbling and feel certain that the salesman's load of merchandise will be lighter by several items before he moves on. Other well-known genre paintings by Ehninger include "The Ford" painted in 1858, "Old Kentucky Home," 1863, and "October," 1867, which may have been painted near Saratoga, New York.

During these years, he also painted some New England landscapes and such historical subjects as an equestrian portrait of George Washington, and the General's first interview with his future wife, Martha Custis. A number of portraits include those of Eastman Johnson and James Renwick. He was also an illustrator of reputation. As early as 1849, he published the illustrations for Hood's "Bridge of Sighs" and, a little less than a decade later, did the illustrations for Longfellow's "Courtship of Miles Standish."

In 1872, rather late in life, he married the granddaughter of Judge Samuel Young of Saratoga, gave up his home in New York, and settled in Saratoga where he lived until his death in 1889. A popular artist in his day, his work was practically forgotten until a few years ago when "Yankee Peddler" and several other canvases were discovered. Today interest in his paintings is keen and one bearing the signature of John Whetton Ehninger and the date is worth owning. Because he was a very prolific artist there are probably a good number of his paintings still to be found. As far as is known, he signed and dated all his pictures.

### A Nineteenth-Century Painter of Outdoor Life

Among the finest of the prints published by Currier & Ives and their contemporaries were reproductions of paintings done by leading artists of the period. Because these artists pictured interesting phases of American life during the years of development and expansion that marked the nineteenth century, both prints and paintings are in favor today, both for their historic importance and their artistic value.

Currier & Ives made a practice of commissioning artists for special work. Several of them were distinguished in their fields. One at least was not over-anxious to have his paintings reproduced as prints. He was Arthur FitzWilliam Tait (1819-1905), painter of sporting and outdoor life. He was born near Liverpool, England, and at the age of fifteen entered the Royal Institute in Manchester. Literally working his way, he was employed by a firm of art dealers by day and at night studied at the Royal Institute by special arrangement.

Tait arrived in New York as a trained artist in 1850. Within three years, he was an associate of the National Academy of Design and by 1858 was admitted to full membership. Between 1852 and 1860, he exhibited over forty canvases there, one of them being "Trappers At Fault, Looking For The Trail" (Illustration 110). Signed and dated "New York, 1852," it shows a prairie landscape.

All of these paintings portrayed some form of outdoor life. The subjects ranged from deer and bear hunting and trout fishing to such homely scenes as maple sugaring in the forest. It is said that Tait's love of nature and the outdoor scene was the driving force that brought him to this country of vast distances where there was ample subject matter for his artistry.

Unlike other painters whose work was reproduced by Currier & Ives, Tait was never in their employ nor was he too easy to get along with. According to the late Harry T. Peters, Tait's correspondence with this firm showed that he was most critical of the way in which his pictures were reproduced and did not much approve of their being reproduced in the first place.

Nevertheless, a good number of them were so done and with such care that today they rank among the best of the Currier & Ives prints. They are mostly in the large-folio size and sold for what was then a good price — a dollar and a half to three dollars. In 1928, one of the rarest of these prints "Life of a Hunter, 'A Tight Fix,'" sold at auction for the record price of three thousand dollars. Other Tait paintings later published as prints include: "Snowed Up, Ruffed Grouse in Winter" which is one of the best of his pictures; "American Forest Scene, Maple Sugaring," dramatizing one of the simple country pleasures of the last century; and "Brook Trout Fishing, 'An Anxious Moment.'"

The painting in Illustration 110 was probably never reproduced as a print. It brought $2,200 at a sale in 1947 at a New York auction gallery. Another painting, "Arguing the Point: Settling the Presidency," by the same artist, sold for nearly a thousand dollars more. It was published as a print in 1855 by N. Currier.

# VII

# Brass and Iron

### Early American Door Knockers

"THE LATCHSTRING IS OUT," is now only a figure of speech, a symbol of hospitality. But the door with a latchstring was a commonplace in early America and continued as part of log-cabin equipment as our forefathers pioneered westward and established new settlements. Then the latchstring was a leather thong attached to a wooden bar on the inside of the door. When passed through a hole to the outside, it served as a latch when pulled. Therefore, a latchstring on the outside was a tacit invitation for the visitor to pull it and enter. When the latchstring was pulled in, the reverse held, of course.

As conditions improved and suitable houses appeared in rapidly growing settlements and towns, social usages became slightly less casual and iron latches and knockers began to adorn the doors of American homes. The village blacksmith who made all the hardware for building and furnishing a house produced latches and knockers too. The earliest type was a ring-shaped device which served the triple purpose of knocker, door-handle, and latch since its pivot released the inside catch. By the early years of the eighteenth century, the separate door handle with latch came into being and the knocker took the place it now has.

Brass later became the favored material, but before the Revolution practically all American-made knockers were of iron, since brass founding was not encouraged in the colonies. Like other brasses, most American-owned knockers were made by the founders of Birmingham, England. These early ones were of the S-shape type. Easy to grasp, resounding and deep in tone, they were popular all through the eighteenth century. They are still a favored design in modern reproductions.

The urn knocker was a fitting ornament for the main door of a fine house in the 1750's. Usually more ornate than the simple example in Illustration 111, left, it reflected the elegance and dignity of the Chippendale period as well as the prosperity of the American colonies. Handsome ones were made of

103

cast iron as well as of brass. The hand-wrought door knocker had been super-seded by those cast in sand molds from models made by wood carvers. This made fanciful design and intricate decoration possible.

Brass knockers were frequently engraved with scrolls and other devices. The owner's initials or his name might also be added as in the illustration. The knocker shown on the right is thus engraved and enameled in block letters which the wayfarer must have been able to see at some distance. Probably made during the first quarter of the nineteenth century, it is a good example of the eagle knocker that was especially popular during the early years of the young Republic. The urn knocker has the owner's monogram in script letters on the center medallion. The date, 1801, appears in an oval on the center of the bail. Both knockers are American-made and indicate the increase in brass founding in this country which began with the close of the American Revolution.

### Brass Candlesticks from Birmingham

Although some of our more opulent ancestors had candlesticks of silver or Sheffield plate, Americans of moderate means felt well served if they had one or more pairs of brass. Kept gleaming by repeated polishings and brought out on special occasions, they were luxuries to be treasured. For everyday use, simpler ones of pewter or wrought iron were adequate.

I well remember a story told me in Vermont, dating back to the 1830's, about a prosperous farmer who was known for his closeness with money and for "liking to put his best foot forward." A young lawyer of some social standing rode up to his house one evening on civic business. As he waited to be admitted after sounding the front door knocker, there were hurried foot-steps within and then came a stage whisper clearly audible to the visitor on the other side of the door.

"Mirandy! Mirandy! Bring in the brass candlesticks. Mr. Samuel Rich-mond's come to call."

Nearly all brass candlesticks in American homes during the candlelight and whale-oil-lamp era were imported from England. In the colonial period, the English Board of Trade had discouraged brass working here, and afterward the brass founders of Birmingham provided such well-designed candlesticks at such reasonable prices that there was little incentive for anyone to produce them in the United States. Hence, brass candlesticks found in America before 1840 were Birmingham-made.

Most of them were of the column type (Illustration 112). The baluster-like shape of the shaft resembled the turnings of some Windsor chairs, indi-cating that the models could well have been made by wood turners. The shaping served a practical purpose too. Since one's fingers fitted well around the narrower rings that separated the bulbous part of the shaft, it could be held firmly when a lighted candle was carried from one place to another. The wide disk of the socket was another practical feature, as it caught the wax that trickled down as the candle burned.

An unseen but ingenious item was the candle ejector. It was a slender iron rod that moved up and down inside the hollow shaft. There was a disk slightly smaller than the candle socket attached to the upper end and another about the size of a dime affixed to the lower end. Slight pressure on this would move the rod up and push the candle stub out. The lower end of the ejector can be seen by looking at the inside base of the stick. Candlesticks complete with ejectors in working order are the most desirable.

Like the cast-brass andirons of the same years, the larger candlesticks were cast in vertical halves and put together by braising. They can be identified by two faint hairlines of lighter color which extend from top to bottom. Breathing on a stick will often make these lines visible. Most Birmingham candlesticks found today date from between 1800 and 1840 when they were at the height of their popularity in America.

### American Animal Weathervanes

In these days of radio weather reports, without which the spot news programs would be considered incomplete, we are apt to forget that there was a time when people had to be their own weather prophets. Would the day be fair and warm or would there be rain by afternoon? Many a citizen prided himself on his ability to sense what sort of weather was imminent.

On-the-spot foretelling of such changes, independent of government weather bureaus, was something farmers and other wise country folk accomplished with surprising accuracy. Knowing how the wind blew was essential, so that a weathervane was a necessity.

During the nineteenth century, hardly a farm was without a vane mounted on the ridge of the big barn or the cupola of a stable. Back in the eighteenth century, weathervanes were mounted on important buildings. Probably the oldest still in use is the arrow vane on the steeple of the First Church in Hartford, Connecticut, placed there in 1737. Another still in place and in the form of a grasshopper is on Faneuil Hall in Boston. Made in 1742, it was the work of Deacon Shem Drowne, a skilled all-around craftsman, born in Kittery, Maine. He is now rated as America's first sculptor. Weathervanes on other public structures were in various forms, such as roosters, bannerettes, and arrows, and were usually sheet-metal silhouettes.

For ordinary farm use, our forebears had to be content with plainer ones of wood, often home-made. They varied from simple arrows that any man handy with a jackknife could whittle out, to larger silhouettes, cut with a scroll-saw from a pine board and mounted on an iron pin.

Such weathervanes were standard for American farms until about 1870, when a three-dimensional type became popular. It appeared on the barns and stables of prosperous farmers and on show buildings of fancy farms owned by financiers, bankers, and railroad titans. The designs were of trotting horses, prize cattle, sheep and hogs, all made with hollow sheet-copper bodies.

The trotting-horse designs with racing sulky and jockey were mostly modeled from Currier & Ives prints of famous winners, such as Flora Temple, Lady Suffolk, still remembered as the beloved Old Gray Mare of folk song, and George M. Patchen, all of whom had established speed records. A few vanes were made in the form of a saddled race horse. The example in Illustration 113 is that of a Morgan stallion hitched to a racing sulky of the period. The peaked cap and sideburn whiskers of the jockey are indicative of the sporting styles of the late nineteenth century. This vane is twenty-five inches long and twelve inches tall.

105

Expensive when new and not cheap when found today, most of these animal vanes were from large city metal shops. Two of the best-known makers, both located in New York, were Fisk and Westervelt.

### American Andirons of Brass and Wrought Iron

From the start of the Colonial period to about 1835 when fireplaces were superseded by stoves, andirons were taken-for-granted household items. For two hundred years American homes depended on wood-burning fireplaces for heat and cooking. Andirons were essential. Probably they were among the necessities brought over by the first settlers.

Just when they were first made here is unknown but those of wrought iron must have been produced for local needs about as soon as the first blacksmiths set up their forges. These artisans played a potent role in the making of America. Home and farm depended on the tools and other necessary items formed on their anvils. In fact, the two evidences that a town was an established community instead of a frontier outpost were a "settled" clergyman and a blacksmith with forge in working order.

The blacksmith made all the fireplace tools and his andirons were of two kinds, those entirely of wrought iron and those with brass uprights and wrought iron leg rests. Most of the brass uprights before the American Revolution were imported from England and then fitted with suitable shafts and log rests by the local blacksmith.

Shapes and patterns in the wrought iron andirons changed little. A simple arch formed the legs. To it a handwrought shaft, sometimes flat and sometimes round, was welded, thus forming the upright which ended in a finial of some sort. There was no effort to form feet with the earlier types. Those dating a little later had a pad-shaped foot, done by hammering when hot. The more decorative of these wrought iron andirons had cast-brass finials of ball and simple urn designs but more were all of iron. A favorite type from about 1750 to 1800 is seen at the right in Illustration 114. Above the arched legs are flat uprights ending in finials known as rose-headed goose-necks, all formed by the skilled hammer of the blacksmith. At the left are a pair of brass andirons of steeple and ball design with spurred legs ending in small ball feet. They date from about 1800.

Brass andiron designs vary, with changing fashions, in foot and upright. The former may be pad, claw and ball, slipper, or simple ball. Uprights include the swirled baluster column, classic urn, and steeple and ball. Those dating from before 1850 are of cast brass made in vertical half sections, braised together, and then smoothed on a lathe. They can be recognized by the fine vertical hairline of the braised joining, usually whiter than the rest. Also the iron support within has a hand-cut thread. Later andirons are of spun brass, have no braising mark, and the interior iron rods have machine-cut threads.

### The Paul Revere Lantern

Lanterns of pierced sheet iron were made in America long before Paul Revere was born. They were a commonplace household article when he was a child. There is no record that the versatile Boston silversmith ever made one but, according to Longfellow's rhymed account of the Patriot's famous ride, he did direct their use as signals from the North Church steeple on that night. So, "one if by land and two if by sea" was enough to give such lanterns the name they have borne for some ninety years or shortly after the poem was published.

They were the sturdiest and least expensive of all the lanterns used by our forefathers. Their design was of European origin and their American manufacture, first of iron and later of tin, began about 1650 and continued until 1825.

Because sheet iron rusts easily if neglected, most of the lanterns which have survived probably date from the early nineteenth century. They were chiefly used by farmers with whom they were especially popular because there was nothing breakable about them. Instead of inset panes of glass or horn, the illumination of the lighted candle within came through almost numberless perforations.

These pierced lanterns vary somewhat in size but an average one is about six inches in diameter by fourteen inches high, not including the ring handle which is attached to the peak of the cone-shaped top by a flexible toggle joint. The base with its central candleholder is slightly larger than the cylindrical body and is attached to it by a crimped edge. The cylinder is about nine inches tall and made of one piece of sheet metal which is lap-joined and riveted. The seam is opposite the rectangular hinged door.

The perforations through which the light shines are usually of two kinds —dot-like punch holes and straight slits about three-quarters of an inch long, made with a small cold chisel. The designs achieved by combining these two kinds of piercing vary. One of the most favored (Illustration 115) consists of four concentric circles of slittings with a punch work center and surrounded by further punch work with single bands of slitting top and bottom. This pattern is repeated three times on the cylinder. Another design, very popular with the Pennsylvania Dutch, has the slit work arranged in a series of round-top arches of diminishing size. This is a single unit pattern, covering the cylinder except for its candle door which is done in a rosette arrangement of slits and punchwork.

These lanterns of sheet iron and, later, of tin have been popular with collectors for many years but are still reasonable in price and can be electrified readily. I have one which has done duty as a hanging hall light for twenty years. I found it at an antique show in Pennsylvania. Before putting it in place, I was curious to see how it worked originally. One breezy night, I inserted a good-sized candle, lighted it, and took the lantern outdoors where I was surprised to find the strong wind had little effect on the candle. It burned evenly and provided ample light for any simple task. Then I deliberately dropped the lantern and the light was promptly extinguished. This seems to me the answer as to why the pierced lanterns were long and widely used. They gave a good light and were foolproof.

### Iron Candlesticks for Common Use

Probably the first settlers in America read or worked after sundown by a flickering rushlight or the murky glow of a betty lamp. By the time their children had homes of their own, there was sufficient leisure for candlemaking to be included in the household chores. Candles were dipped or molded from tallow or beeswax and holders for them were in demand.

Various inventories of estates in the latter part of the seventeenth century mention candlesticks. These were of pewter and brass for the moderately well-to-do and of silver for the mansions of merchants. For everyday home use, householders relied on the wrought iron stick, hammered out on the anvil of the local blacksmith.

Like the four candlesticks in Illustration 116, they were simple in form, just a cylindrical column attached to a circular base. One side of the column was an iron spur which slid up and down in a slot, thus raising the candle as it grew shorter. Some of the candlesticks had a broad base with a loop handle on one side, like the one at center right which was found in Virginia. They were intended for bedrooms and for carrying from room to room. The neatly formed candle snuffer in front of this Virginia stick is of steel and probably came from Sheffield, England.

Probably the most interesting as a symbol of early American life are the three candlesticks at right and left, called "hog-scrapers" because of the circular base with sharp edge. This made such a stick a very adaptable piece of household gear. The primary use was that of a lighting device but the sharp-edged base lent itself neatly to barbering a freshly killed hog. In addition, the rim at the top of the column usually had a hook on one side which enabled one to hang the candlestick either on a shelf edge or on the back of a chair when a light for reading or working was wanted. It was ingenious but risky as charred spots often appearing on an old slat-back chair indicate.

Candlesticks so designed originated in England in the eighteenth century and were made there and in America until well into the 1800's. Being utilitarian everyday pieces of cheap and plentiful native iron, few if any of those made in the early colonial years have survivived. Most of those found today date from about 1790 to 1830 when tin began to replace wrought iron for candlesticks.

Less common but still in existence are the tripod-base floor candlesticks, ancestors of the modern floor lamp. With these, the candleholders were designed to be moved up and down as desired. Examples with only one socket were probably intended for workshop rather than home use. I know of one two-socket example that may well have stood in the best room of a comfortably furnished eighteenth-century house. Its delicately formed finial and other decorative details show what a good craftsman could do with humble material.

These wrought iron candlesticks are of interest to students and collectors of early lighting devices. They are also not without merit for the present-day country home.

### Tin Sconces

Candlelight was the chief means of lighting American homes before the advent of various types of whale-oil and kerosene lamps. Whale-oil lamps first appeared about 1815. Those using kerosene, at first called "coal oil," did not come into general use until several years after the discovery of petroleum in 1859.

Candles continued to hold their own during most of the 1860's, especially in rural sections. They gave no more light then than now, so to supplement those used in various kinds of candlesticks, there was widespread use of wall sconces. The majority were of tin, but a merchant or a wealthy land owner might have a pair or two made of silver for the best rooms.

Just how early such sconces were used in American homes is not known definitely, probably about 1700. The first ones were imported from England, were expensive, and few in number. Then in 1740, William and Andrew Patterson emigrated from Ireland and opened a tinsmith's shop in Berlin, Connecticut. Other tinsmiths opened shops elsewhere in that colony and in such Massachusetts towns as Dedham and Hingham. Working with sheets of tin plate about two feet square, imported from England and known as "best charcoal tin," these tinsmiths made a wide variety of lanterns, sconces, and candlesticks, as well as plates, teakettles, and coffee pots which they supplied to tin peddlers.

These peddlers, from early spring until late fall, followed their routes through the farming country. They first traveled on foot, carrying their wares in large baskets on their shoulders. Later came the picturesque tin peddler with horse-drawn cart piled high with an assortment of tin wares, mainly candlesticks, sconces, and lanterns. Many of the peddlers came from Connecticut and since, by the early nineteenth century, they were often away from home for months at a time, warehouses where they could restock their wagons were established in such cities as Albany, New York, Philadelphia, Richmond, Charleston, and Cincinnati.

The sconces and candlesticks were usually simplified copies of more expensive ones of silver or brass. The first sconces were of the tall oblong type, like the two at right and left in Illustration 117. These were made from about 1760 to 1830. The more elaborate circular or shield-shaped sconces, often with inserts of mirror glass to aid in reflecting the light of the candle flame, date from a little after 1800 to about 1850. This particular circular pair was assembled from a stock of parts found in a long-disused tinsmith's shop at Willimantic, Connecticut. They were made about 1840 or possibly later. Both the oblong and the circular pairs are good examples of the simpler types made by American tinsmiths. The oblong pair are eleven inches tall by three and one-half inches wide. The circular ones are six and one-half inches in diameter and have central mirror glass insets, two inches in diameter. The small covered pot below them was used to refill whale-oil lamps.

### Coach Lamps

For about fifty years, state laws have required vehicles to be lighted from sunset to sunrise. Before the motor-car era, whether a coach or carriage was fitted with lamps was a matter of the owner's preference. Then eight miles an hour was a fast pace. Night traffic was at a minimum and lighting one's carriage was not considered essential to public safety.

Yet coach and carriage lamps came into use quite early in the nineteenth century, and after 1825, as highways improved and cities grew larger, operators of stage coaches and affluent citizens who kept their own carriages began to equip their vehicles with side lights.

Dim as these lights were by present day standards, they were satisfactory to nineteenth-century eyes and their popularity grew. From about 1850 on, stage coaches, such as those first made at Concord, New Hampshire, and known as a Concord coaches in the East and as an Overland Mail coach further west, were not fully equipped without a pair of lamps placed just back of the driver's seat on projecting brackets. So it was also with the enclosed carriage for city use, whether a four-wheeled hired hackney, a two-wheeled hansom cab, or such private carriages as a brougham, landau, or barouche.

As the fashion grew, these lamps became larger and more elaborate. Their design was basically derived from the enclosed torch, sometimes called a link, in use in Europe during the eighteenth century and earlier. What had been the staff carried by a link-boy became the hollow container for fuel which, after 1859, was kerosene. Many of the lamps were elaborate in design and decoration (Illustration 118). They were usually of sheet iron, japanned black, and often trimmed with bands of Sheffield plate. There was glass on the front and on the outer side. The interior was of Sheffield or other silver plate for reflecting the light.

Many of the largest lamps were used on hearses or on the delivery wagons of department stores of the luxury class—some silver plated with the lantern part eight-sided and panes of glass all around. For simpler carriages, such as the buggy in which many a country doctor made his rounds, the lamps were smaller and more lantern-like. Occasionally, one sees an elaborate pair of brass lamps with a number in red, blue, or green on the glass. These were made for an early voluntary fire-company apparatus.

Most carriage and coach lamps found in good condition today date from about 1865 to 1890. They are now collector's items, much in demand as lights for the front doors of country and suburban homes. Electrified, they give a graceful touch to a doorway and shed much more light then they ever did when mounted on the sides of a carriage or coach.

# VIII

# Pewter

## *Pewter-Making in the Nineteenth Century*

ONE OF THE first indications of easier living in the American colonies was the use of pewter for household items. It was the first step up from the wooden trencher for table use and from the wrought iron candlestick which served to light the hardworking pioneer to his night's rest.

By the eighteenth century, pewter was taken for granted by all except the very rich or very poor. The latter still had to do with bare necessities; the rich were able to provide the growing number of silversmiths with a good living. While pewterers had to serve apprenticeships just as silversmiths, the training was about half as long. Pewter, being a soft alloy, was much easier to work.

Since pewter took the place of the more costly silverware for the man of moderate means, it followed the same style patterns and was made in the same forms. Pewterers, like silversmiths, marked their wares. In England they were subject to guild regulations which involved quality and touch marks. American pewterers were bound by none of these rules legally, but by tradition and habit each craftsman adopted individual touch marks which he impressed on a finished piece in an inconspicuous place—the bottom of a tankard, plate, or teapot, or on the underside of a lid. It might be a name, two or more initials, or a series of marks in the English manner with the maker's initials.

The eighteenth century was the age of pewter, as far as quality and variety of pieces were concerned. Comparatively few of the large number of pieces made during this period have survived. Pewter being a perishable alloy, articles made of it were easily ruined by close contact with heat and by hard daily use. Yet, except for cooking utensils, practically every sort of household and personal accessory was made in pewter.

111

It was used for all kinds of tableware, candlesticks, whale-oil lamps, snuff boxes, inkwells and sanders, desk boxes, pocket flasks, buttons, buckles, spectacle cases, and miniature frames. The makers of these articles ranged from accomplished craftsmen to the lowly traveling tinker who went from house to house with his spoon mold, and was glad to convert broken bits of the alloy into a dozen spoons for a few pennies and a night's lodging.

The desk box in Illustration 119 was made by Henry Will, a New York pewterer who worked at his trade from 1765 to 1793. The box, made for holding pens, ink, and sander, has the maker's touch mark on the raised lid of one of the compartments—a crowned rose below four square reserves of an animal's head, a female figure, a lion rampant, and the initials "H. W." Henry Will evidently had other business interests besides pewter. In 1770, he advertised the sale of a glue house, adding, "For further particulars, inquire of Henry Will, Pewterer, who makes, sells, and exchanges all sorts of Pewter Ware." In 1776, he advertised his removal to Albany to carry on his pewtering business there. His kinsman, Colonel William Will of Philadelphia, who is credited with making the ink well used at the signing of the Declaration of Independence, kept an inn to bolster his income. Either the craft was not profitable enough or the thrifty workers believed in more than one calling.

The finest American tankards were made about 1720 and continued in favor until about 1840. Some of them had the domed top (Illustration 120); others were made with a flat top. There were also tankards without covers, usually known as mugs. They were for ale and similar beverages and were common in both private homes and taverns. Their designs were similar to those used by the silversmiths of the period.

Since pewterers marked their wares, it is possible to date surviving examples of their work today. The five tankards in the illustration were made between 1750 and 1800 and represent the work of such eighteenth-century craftsmen as William Will of Philadelphia, David Melville of Newport, and John Will, Frederick and John Bassett, all of New York.

### Jumbo Pewter Plates

The first generation of American colonists lived in rude shelters and ate from wooden trenchers. But they didn't remain in that state any longer than they could help. Their trust in Divine Providence, hard work, and good business sense soon brought prosperity to a considerable number. Living conditions improved and home comforts multiplied.

By the middle of the seventeenth century, importations from the mother country included sizable amounts of pewter dishes for table use. This alloy of tin, copper, and antimony was relatively cheap, its value being only six-pence the pound as against silver at twenty-five shillings per ounce, troy weight. A man of means could well afford a good quantity of pewter for household use.

That practically no pewter dating back to the seventeenth century has survived is not surprising since it was put to general use, much as glass and earthenware are today. Because of the softness of the alloy, eight to ten years was about the span of an article's usefulness. Then it was taken to the local pewterer to be melted down and made into a new form.

(*Illustration 117*) American Tin Sconces, ca. 1760-1830.

*(Illustration 118)* Carriage Lamps with Silver Mounts.

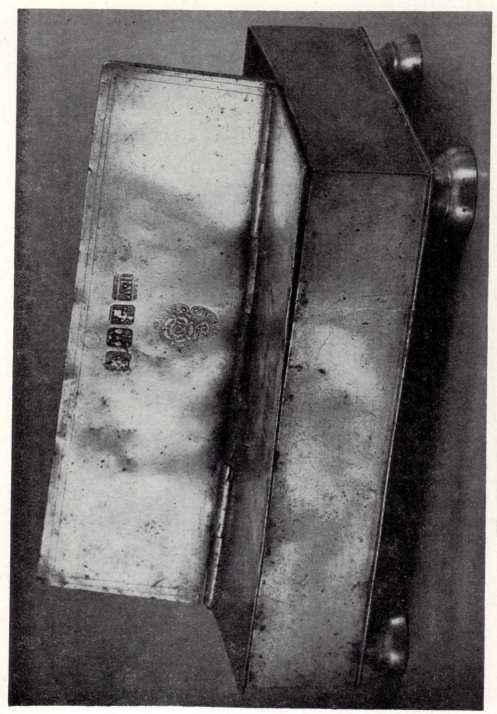

*(Illustration 119)* Pewter Desk Box, by Henry Will, ca. 1770.

*(Illustration 120)* American Pewter Tankards and, center, a Mug, ca. 1750-1800.

*(Illustration 121a)* Large American Pewter Plate, by Simon Edgell, Philadelphia, Eighteenth Century.

*(Illustration 121b)* Eighteenth-Century American Pewter Salver. Unidentified maker, but marked LQNDON.

*(Illustration 122)* Covered Pewter Pitcher, Marked "Boardman & Hart, N. York," ca. 1827.

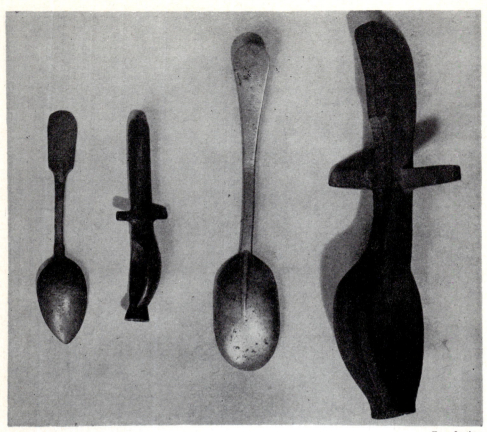

*(Illustration 123)* **Pewter Spoons and Molds.**

*(Illustration 124)* **Woven Blue-and-White Coverlet, Dated July 4, 1826, by Elijah Northrup.**

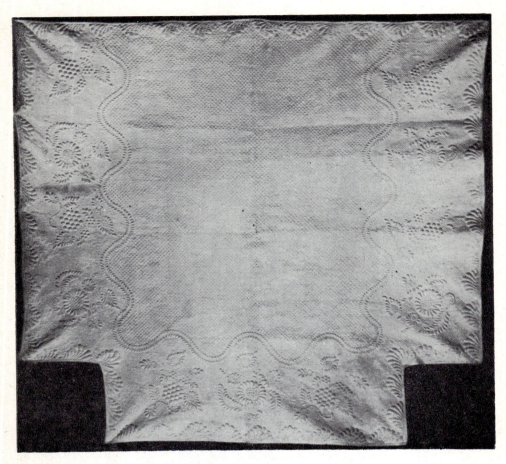

*(Illustration 125)* All-White, Hand-Quilted and Stuffed Coverlet, Dated 1819.

*(Illustration 126)* "Star of Bethlehem" Patchwork Quilt, ca. 1830.

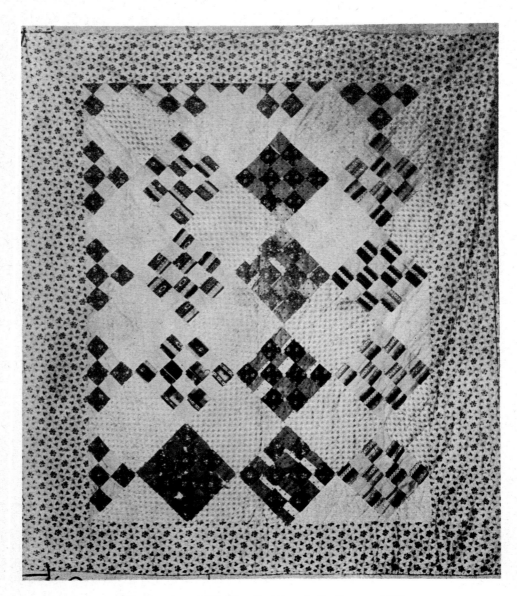

*(Illustration 127)* Simple Pieced Quilt, ca. 1850.

*(Illustration 128)* **Wallpaper-Covered Bandbox, ca. 1835.**

*(Illustration 129)* **Small Trunk Covered with Wallpaper.**

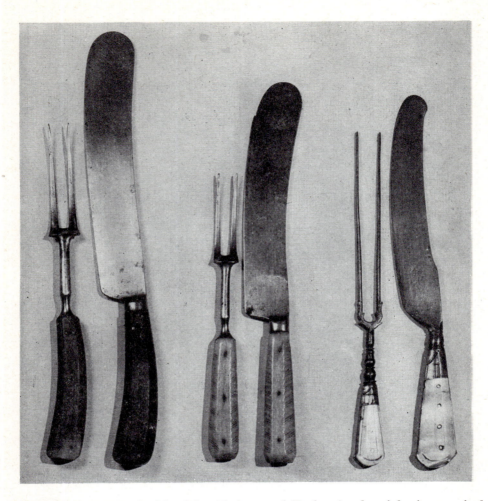

*(Illustration 130)* **Early Matching Knives and Forks. At the right is a typical seventeenth-century set with pearl handles, long-pronged fork, and shaped knife blade. The sets at the left and center are eighteenth-century. Note the shorter tined forks and the handles of wood or bone.**

(*Illustration 131*) American Nineteenth-Century Chopping Bowls.

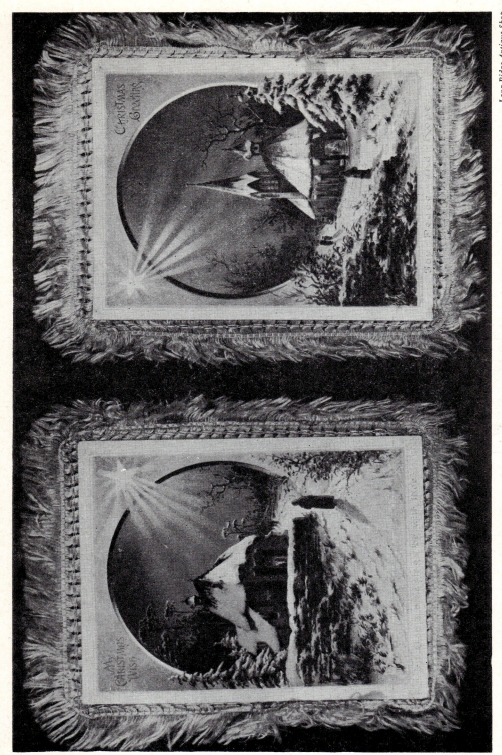

*(Illustration 132)* **American Double-faced Christmas Card, ca. 1885.**

Probably the first pewterers in America were simply repairers and importers. But by the start of the eighteenth century, a fair number were established whose wares could compare successfully with English importations. These men followed the styles of their brethren across the water and even marked their wares in similar manner. Plates, of course, were among the important table furnishings and varied from the six and eight-inch size for individual use to the salvers of twelve to twenty-seven inches in diameter. The latter were serving dishes, were fairly expensive, and evidently received better care since quite a few are still in existence.

The salver shown in Illustration 121a was made in Philadelphia by an early pewterer named Simon Edgell. He worked there between 1713 and 1742, was English, and followed the tradition of his native land in his manner of working and in marking his wares. His touch mark was that of a bird with three pellets beneath and his name spelled in capital letters in an oblong below. Sometimes the name "Philadelphia" also appears. Pewter plates were cast in a disc-like mold and then hammered into shape by the craftsman on a polished steel stake similar to that used by silversmiths. The upper side was then polished with sand and brick dust against a buffing wheel which erased the hammer marks, at least on the small plates. But the marks are still apt to show on the larger plates, as on the Edgell salver.

Importations of British-made pewter continued to compete with that made by native craftsmen and some of the latter apparently sought to remedy this by deceptive marking. The other salver in Illustration 121b has a rose-and-crown touch mark, a device used in both England and America by various pewterers. It bears no maker's name but has "LQNDON" in an oblong. The unknown pewterer could claim this as his mark, and if the unwary happened to read it "LONDON," it was no concern of his.

A seventeenth-century pewter salver is most desirable. Such pieces are quite rare but they do show up occasionally. Some years ago I found a twenty-four-inch one in the shop of a New England antiques repairer. It was black with age and neglect and it took much prolonged and patient cleaning to bring back its soft sheen and discover the touch mark on the under side. It proved to be the work of Sir John Fryers who was Master of the London Pewterers Company in 1694.

### The Boardmans, Pewterers

Any piece of pewter bearing one of the several Boardman touch marks is an example of the well-designed work done in Connecticut during the second quarter of the nineteenth century. There were four Boardman brothers and back of them was a long tradition of family pewtering through their mother, Sarah Danforth, who married Oliver Boardman of Hartford in 1781. She was a granddaughter of Thomas Danforth, one of the best known of eighteenth-century American pewterers and ancestor of a considerable group who followed the same trade for another two generations.

It is generally conceded that Oliver and Sarah's four sons, Thomas Danforth, Sherman, Timothy, and Henry, all learned the craft of pewtermaking from one or another of their Danforth uncles. The eldest, Thomas Danforth

Boardman, had his own shop on Main Street about 1825. He marked his pieces "T. D. Boardman, Hartford," sometimes combined with the impress of an eagle or a lion. He was presently joined by his brother Sherman. Their usual mark was "T D & S B," impressed block-letter initials in a rectangle. This mark was used until about 1854. They had a large, well-organized factory and were probably the first pewterers to be established on such a scale.

With their sizable output, they had to devise better ways of marketing it than the old method of selling it to itinerant peddlers. The answer proved to be establishments in New York and Philadelphia where the wares made in Hartford were sold, with special distinguishing marks for each branch.

For instance, brother Timothy went to New York about 1825 where he first did business as "Boardman & Company" with his pewter so marked. In about a year, the firm name was changed to "Boardman & Hart, N-York" and the touch mark accordingly. Shortly afterward, Timothy Boardman ceased to be active in New York but Lucius Hart continued the business on Wall Street until 1850. The covered pitcher in Illustration 122 bears the Boardman & Hart mark. An early piece, it probably dates from before 1830. It is in the two-quart size and fashioned in the pleasing design characteristic of the Hartford pewterers.

The fourth brother, Henry S. Boardman, went to Philadelphia in 1844. Three years before, he had been listed in Hartford as a working pewterer with a shop on Trumbull Street. The Philadelphia business was organized as Boardman & Hall. The touch mark was the firm name with "Phlad'a" impressed beneath. The style, but not the touch mark, was changed in about a year to Hall, Boardman & Co. and, in 1849, to Hall & Boardman. The latter was retained until the branch was closed in 1853.

Close relationship between the Hartford factory and the branches in New York and Philadelphia is indicated by occasional pieces that are found where the mark, "Boardman & Hall," has been partially erased and altered to "Boardman & Hart," or the other way around. Evidently some workman used the wrong second name.

The Boardmans made a wide range of articles, including plates, porringers, and mugs, but were especially successful in the pleasing shape of their hollow ware pieces, such as open and covered pitchers of up to gallon size, teapots, coffee pots, and communion flagons. These followed the lines of the earlier domed tankards.

### Pewter Spoons and Their Making

Pewter spoons were important items in the American home for nearly two hundred years. Wills probated only twenty years after the first colonist landed in Massachusetts listed pewter spoons. Toward the close of the seventeeth century, a sizable quantity was being imported from England and there were also a number of pewterers working in America, all of whom presumably made spoons along with other household articles in this alloy.

The earliest known piece of marked American pewter is a spoon. It was dug up some years ago at Jamestown, Virginia, and bears on its handle the name of Joseph Copeland of Chuckatuck and the date, 1677. Copeland was a

London-trained pewterer who apparently migrated to Virginia shortly after he had served his apprenticeship. He may or may not have made anything besides spoons. Household pewter was made for common use and, though quantities were produced, comparatively few pieces made before the nineteenth century have survived. This is especially true of spoons. In fact, what saved the Copeland for twentieth-century eyes was probably its accidental interment.

Pewter followed the styles of silver but in spoon-making the methods were quite different. The process of turning a strip of silver into a spoon was lengthy. It involved repeated heatings, shapings with anvil and hammer, filings, and burnishings. This ran into time and money. Consequently, a man who owned a few silver spoons was considered well-to-do and only the wealthy could afford a good supply of both spoons and hollow ware.

Since pewter is soft metal, spoons made of it were formed in a mold. These molds were of brass, bronze, bell metal, or iron. They were in two parts and were held together by a clamp (Illustration 123). The molten metal was poured into it and, when formed and cool, was removed in the shape of a spoon. The edges were then scraped and the piece burnished and polished. These finishing steps were, of course, all done by hand.

Decorative elements were the result of designs cut into the mold. Spoons made by trained pewterers were naturally better finished and their molds of good quality and design. In addition to spoons from their shops, many others were made at home out of old pewter, broken pieces and the like. One spoon mold in a community was freely loaned by its owner to any neighbor who had some old pewter and was thrifty enough to convert it into spoons.

There were also the early nineteenth-century tinkers who traveled the countryside on foot carrying their molds and other tools with them. They made an indifferent living, according to the record of one who kept a journal. In it, he told of melting some old pewter plates, running the resulting metal in his spoon mold, and so making and finishing twelve spoons. For this entire process, he received thirty cents.

Braziers and brass and iron foundries were, of course, the makers of these spoon molds, but if they advertised them it is lost information. Old spoon molds are to be found in museums and private collections. In fact, there are pewter collectors owning such molds who like to use broken and hopelessly damaged pieces as material for running spoons. Such spoons can not be classed as old, but they make a good addition to a table setting of this once-lowly household ware.

# IX

# Quilts and Coverlets

### Coverlets, Dated and Otherwise

ALONG WITH patchwork quilts, the weaving of coverlets started in America in the eighteenth century. Weaving such coverlets was originally just another of the endless number of household tasks that housewives undertook as part of their workaday activities. The chief materials were home grown.

From the field of flax came the undyed linen yarn used for the warp to form the white background of the coverlet pattern as it was woven on an overshot hand loom. The wool was sheared from the family's flock of sheep, then cleansed, carded, and spun on a wheel into the yarn. But before the actual work of weaving, this wool had to be dyed the desired color. This was also home-done in large kettles outdoors. Indigo was used for blue, madder and a variety of leaves and tree barks for the other colors.

The overshot loom was a cumbersome affair with timber frames about as large as four-poster bed. Sometimes it stood in the corner of a large living-room-kitchen of the farmhouse. In a more elaborate household, there might be a special weaving room in the attic or over a shed. Weaving of coverlets persisted until just a few years ago in the cabins of many southern mountaineers. On such looms were woven the simple geometric patterns known as "Queen's Fancy," "Braddock's Defeat," and "Morning Star." Many such patterns continued in favor for well over a century.

As demand for more elaborate patterns manifested itself, the itinerant weaver appeared on the American scene. These traveling weavers were well established by the outbreak of the American Revolution. Often they had learned their trade in England or on the Continent before migrating to America. Skilled workers, they wove the more elaborate double-weave coverlets that were done in such geometric patterns as "Irish Chain" and "Wheel of Fortune."

The final step in coverlet weaving came with the Jacquard loom, about 1820. Invented by the Frenchman whose name it bears, this loom made it possible to weave coverlets with floral, leaf, bird, and other intricate patterns. As far as is known, some of the first weavers to use Jacquard looms worked in New York State. One of the best known was Archibald Davidson of Ithaca. He generally wove his name in the border so his coverlets are easy to identify.

Another weaver was Elijah Northrup of Roanoke, New York. The example in Illustration 124 shows a typical Northrup design with a conventionalized center of repeated floral and leafage motifs while the border combines such patriotic details as Independence Hall, the Liberty Bell, and the spread eagle from the coat of arms of the United States. Northrup sometimes, as here, added Masonic emblems, such as the square and compass and twin columns. He usually wove the name of the person for whom the coverlet had been made and the date in the corners. Sometimes he wove a patriotic slogan in the corners and then repeated the name of the owner four times on either end.

This particular Northrup coverlet was done in blue and white. In addition to the characteristic border, he added the following slogan in the four corners: "Agriculture & Manufactures Are the Foundation of Our Independence, July 4, 1826, Gen'l Lafayette." This celebrates Lafayette's visit to America in that year. According to his usual custom, Northrup also wove the owner's name, E. Washburn, four times on either end.

### The Hand-Quilted Coverlet

Quilting was undoubtedly among the forms of needlework practiced by early American housewives from the days of the Plymouth settlement until well into the second half of the nineteenth century. The art of quilting developed along with weaving, spinning, and crewel embroidery until, by 1750, quilts were commonplace articles in the average household.

There were various types and the designs were numerous. Whatever the design, three parts were necessary—top, lining, and interlining, all joined together by finely set stitches in a definite pattern. There were also three ways to make the top. There could be a plain piece of cloth with the decoration depending entirely on the quilting design (Illustration 125). There could be a plain piece of cloth overlaid with a design of patchwork, or there could be a top made of cloth fragments pieced together in blocks of varied size, color, and shape. The latter was really a product of the maker's spare time and the contents of her piece bag which held every scrap left over from the making of clothes.

The pieced quilt was strictly for everyday use and the quilting design was relatively simple. The patchwork top, on the other hand, provided a real chance for artistic expression and many of the designs resembled crewel work with cloth instead of thread as a medium.

But for intricacy of quilting, there was nothing like the all-white coverlet. It had a very thin interlining and the special quilting design usually consisted of a large central panel or pattern with smaller ones in harmony for the corners. Every inch of the material was quilted, even to the background which resembled a woven fabric.

117

As a finishing touch, after the coverlet was removed from the quilting frame, the main design was often brought into relief by stuffing the most prominent features. To do this, tiny holes were made on the wrong side and cotton pushed in with a large needle until every detail so treated stood out in bold relief. The example in the illustration has a border, notched at the lower corners to fit a four-poster, quilted in a shell and floral pattern. The central panel is quilted so minutely as to resemble petitpoint. On the reverse, in stitching, is the inscription, "Quilted by Mrs. Eunice Ely and her daughter, Catherine, in Chester, Conn., in 1819 and stuffed by the latter."

The idea for this kind of coverlet may well have stemmed from a type of counterpane known during the Elizabethan period in England which was worked in geometric figures. In America, the all-white coverlet was in vogue from the latter years of the eighteenth through the first quarter of the nineteenth centuries.

Today surviving examples are very rare. Machine-made imitations, known as Marseilles bedspreads, were popular during the 1890's, and even into the present century, but are not to be confused with the fine hand-wrought coverlet of a century earlier.

### The Patchwork Quilt and the Star Design

Patchwork and quilting are two of the oldest forms of needlework. Both were used in the colorful bed coverings favored as counterpanes in America from 1775 to about 1870, when starched pillow shams and Marseilles spreads became the fashion for the well-appointed bedroom.

Known as patchwork quilts, the designs were set in a white background of either linen or, after 1810, of cotton. The patterns were mostly geometric and their names were many. Those based on the star were the most popular. Five-pointed and set in a five-sided background which was framed by a circle, it was a compass pattern; six-pointed, it appeared in a triple six-sided design; and as eight-pointed, it was used in a number of ways.

A very arresting design was that of the large central star (Illustration 126). Known as "Star of Bethlehem," it could appear singly against a white background or be surrounded by smaller stars or sunbursts, with or without floral appliqués. The maker of the quilt illustrated was content with a single large star made up of diamond-shaped pieces of calico in various colors. Double diamond patches form a neat and pleasing design in the border. A fine example of intricate patchwork, this quilt dates from between 1820 and 1840. The close random stitch was used for the quilting.

Patchwork quilts were tests of skill and patience on the part of needle-women. For a "Star of Bethlehem," over a thousand diamond-shaped pieces of calico had to be carefully cut out and joined so that from a small central star they spread out in sunburst effect to form the large eight-pointed star of many colors. This was then set, like a patch, in the white background. The quilt was then ready for lining and interlining, after which it was put on a frame for the quilting bee. "Star of Bethlehem" quilts date from as early as 1775, but few examples made before 1820 will be found in good condition. The design remained popular to the middle of the nineteenth century and is the most important pattern found today.

From a decorative point of view, the height of quilt making was reached during the first half of the nineteenth century and many fine examples have survived in good condition. As with other forms of folk art they reflected the political, social, and economic affairs of their time and were named accordingly. Such names as "Whig Rose," "Wagon Tracks," "Dolly Madison's Star," "Road to California," and 'Texas Star" recall events in American history and help to date the pattern, though not always the quilt.

### Early American Pieced Quilts

Although both patchwork and pieced quilts are prized today for their designs and fine needlework, they were originally a product of spare time and thrift. The earliest quilts in America were probably of wool and done in that oldest of designs, the "crazy" pattern, with warmth rather than beauty the object.

Wool quilts with pieced tops in the simplest of block patterns were made all through the colonial days and until late in the nineteenth century. Some of them had artistic merit. I know of one made in the 1850's with squares of challis in quaint floral and striped patterns which now has the mellow charm of an antique prayer rug. Lined with lamb's wool and still in perfect condition, it has beauty as well as warmth.

The pieced quilt was a result of the frugal habit of using left-overs. It is reminiscent of an era when women's and children's clothes were made at home, either by a clever member of the family or by the local seamstress who appeared as regularly as spring and fall house-cleaning, reigned in an upper room for a week and then departed, leaving an array of feminine raiment and an assortment of cloth scraps.

These by-products were sorted, tied in little bundles, and put into a piece bag. Sizable pieces of calico, India print, gingham, or other colorful cottons were for the handsome patchwork or appliqué type of quilt; smaller odds and ends were earmarked for the pieced blocks of the everyday quilts (Illustration 127).

Since pieced blocks are always divisions of either a square or a circle, many of the patterns commonly used by the quilt-maker of yesterday and today are as old as the science of mathematics. For the cotton pieced quilt of elaborate design, patterns ranged from sunburst, star, and log cabin to simple geometric ones.

Squares like those of the quilt in the illustration were often used for a little girl's first lessons in sewing a fine seam. Tiny over-and-over stitches with sixteen squares to a block might take much or little time. From this beginning, the pupil would presumably progress to more intricate designs until she was promoted to the aristocratic quilt of patchwork. Finally, she became sufficiently advanced in skill to take part in the actual quilting.

The latter called for a party, and as not over eight women could work on a quilt at the same time, a smart hostess waited until she had two or three quilts ready and so paid off a good number of social obligations.

119

# X

# Miscellaneous

### *Wallpaper-Covered Luggage*

TODAY IF YOU SEE a photogenic young women with a hat box of shiny black looped over her arm as she walks down a busy street, it's a safe guess that she is a professional model hurrying from one appointment to another. A hundred years and more ago, before Daguerre had invented the first form of the camera, such feminine hand luggage was more colorful and decorative.

Whether in the form of a capacious bandbox or a miniature trunk, the covering was bright-colored wallpaper. Largely imported from England and France, it came in sheets ten by nineteen inches. The designs reflected the life of the time. Some showed sporting prints, others, American views, such as a balloon ascension at Sandy Hook or the Battery, New York. The newly invented steamboat and railway engine were also pictorial subjects.

Most of these old bandboxes still in existence date from about 1825 to just before the Civil War. They were made in three sizes and were oval in shape. The large size measured twenty-four by eighteen inches, the medium twenty by sixteen inches, and the small size eighteen by fourteen inches. Top and bottom were usually of thin wood and the sides of cardboard. Some were entirely of cardboard. They were lined either with plain white paper or newspaper. The latter, being cheaper, was widely used and serves today for dating a box so lined.

Bandboxes were made and sold by firms in several cities—New York, Philadelphia, York and Lancaster, Pennsylvania, and Hartford, Connecticut. The bandbox in Illustration 128 was made in the latter city about 1834. The patriotic design is in red, white, and blue with the American eagle standing on a box lettered "Hartford, Conn.," and the ribbon in its mouth is inscribed with the name of the makers, "Putnam and Roff, Paper Hanging & Band Box Manufac."

This form of feminine luggage was apparently more popular in America than the small trunks which enjoyed considerable favor in England. None of the trunks date much later than 1830 and are consequently rarer. The example in Illustration 129 is the earliest that I have seen. It is lined with a page of the *Hartford Courant* for July 3, 1811. It is in almost perfect condition, despite its age.

How much care was taken in applying the paper to make the most of its hand-blocked and hand-colored design in green and old rose can be seen on the front. Here the pattern continues without a break over the curved top. The shape is very old. With its curved top, it follows the lines of much larger wooden ·chests made in Europe as early as the fifteenth century. It is also a forerunner of that American institution, the Saratoga trunk of the 1870's. The body of this little trunk is basswood with dovetailed corners. The lid is attached with a pair of wire snipe hinges and there are leather straps at the sides to keep it vertical when raised.

### Early Knives and Forks

Eating tools are of comparatively recent date. Even at the time of the discovery of America, the ewer and basin, ancestors of the modern finger bowl, were necessary items at the end of a meal. Forks were especially late in appearing on the dining table, though Italians were using a small two-pronged utensil by the middle of the fifteenth century. It reached England about 1610 when it was at first considered a silly piece of Continental foppery.

Gradually the British viewed the new implement with less alarm and it became an established piece of tableware. One of the earliest forms was the sucket fork, used for sweetmeats. Made of silver, it had a rounded spoonbowl at one end and a short two-pronged fork at the other. English and American silversmiths produced these combination tools through most of the seventeenth century. Not many American-made sucket forks are still in existence. Probably few were made, since they were among the luxuries ordered by those wealthy colonists who could pay for them.

Steel knives with matching two-pronged forks, on the other hand, were made in England for some years before the first colonists set sail for America. They had decorative handles, much like those shown at the right (Illustration 130), and each set was provided with a leather case so that the owner might have them at hand when he ate away from home.

Incidentally, the early fork with its sharp prongs was designed for holding the meat when cutting it; the knife of the same period had a wide upcurved tip for carrying food to the mouth. So began a socially correct custom of eating with the knife which continued in the United States until nearly the middle of the nineteenth century and persisted even longer in rural areas.

During these years, most English and American tables were furnished with knives and forks of steel, usually bearing the marks of some Sheffield cutlery manufacturer. The forks were made with two fairly short prongs and the knife blades had the wide curving tip suited for use as feeding tools. The handles might be bone, horn, or hard close-grained wood.

The maker's mark was stamped on the knife blade rather near the handle. Practically all were those of English cutlers. Old steel is anything but stainless, so years of daily scouring and frequent sharpenings have had their effect on

121

these marks. Today the majority are only partially visible. Those showing a legible mark, such as Barton Brothers, Sheffield, are apt to be of the late eighteenth or early nineteenth century.

By that time, the three-pronged fork had appeared and the knife blade had less the outline of a feeding tool. After 1850, steel knives and forks took on the shape still in use today. They also bore the marks of American cutlers to some extent. Today they are in special favor for informal table settings on porch or terrace.

### Early American Wooden Ware

The first American settlers were not burdened with the care of fine china, silver, or even glass for their table settings. Nor had they been accustomed to them in the homes they had left. They lived in an age of wood. Among the few material things they brought with them were square wooden plates, known as trenchers, and platters, bowls, and spoons.

In the new land, plenty of wood was to be had for the taking and after the first rude shelters were built, each householder could set about adding to this assortment of table and kitchen ware. American-made trenchers were round, done on that very old tool, the lathe. Dishes of shapes that could not be so fashioned were executed by hand with knife and adze.

Because all these wooden dishes were more or less handmade and not too plentiful, a change of plates consisted of turning one's trencher over and using the reverse side, a custom brought from early seventeenth-century England where the square trencher had such effete details as a hollowed out center for food, an indentation in one corner for salt, and quite often a lettered inscription as a finish around the square. This survives today in the "Give us this day our daily bread" inscriptions on bread plates of glass, china, or wood.

Other wooden tableware included bowls of various sizes from the salt dish to the large one, either round or oval, which held the main dish of the meal; wooden mugs, known as noggins, used as the common drinking cup in an age when the word "germ" was unknown; and bread boards, used for slicing the loaf of bread at the table.

Possibly the greatest variety occurred in bowls. Their usefulness was not confined to the table since they also did duty as working tools, especially the large sizes which were used either as chopping bowls or as serving dishes. There were also wash bowls, shaped like the earthenware ones of later date. Woods used for these bowls included maple, birch, walnut, cherry, and sometimes lignum-vitae, brought back from the West Indies and fashioned into bowls by sailors in their spare time.

The two bowls in Illustration 131 date from the early nineteenth century. The circular one is of straight-grained maple, over eighteen inches in diameter and five inches deep, and made on a lathe. Marks of the chopping knife are visible. The oblong bowl is all hand-done with such tools as draw-shave, chisel and, for the inside, a plane with curved face. It is made from the heart of a yellow birch. Its flaring sides were cut down to a flat bottom, the interior shaped, and finally a coat of red paint applied to the outside. It still retains much of its original finish.

## Louis Prang and the Christmas Card

The general exchange of Christmas cards, taken for granted today, dates back only a little over three decades. Louis Prang is sometimes called the father of the Christmas card. This Boston originator of chromolithography was born in Breslau, Germany, in 1824, the son of a calico manufacturer.

Trained as a colorist, he did creditable work in this phase of textile manufacture until the late 1840's, when he found himself on the losing side of a German revolution and was forced to leave hurriedly for Bohemia, then for Switzerland, and thence to America. He landed in New York in April, 1850, found no work there, moved on to New England, and settled in Boston where he took up wood engraving as a business.

Years of unlucky partnerships followed until 1860 when the firm name became L. Prang & Co., the silent partner being his wife, Rosa. Within the next decade, he perfected his process of lithographic printing in full colors and eventually became one of America's important publishers of "chromos," as he named them. He intended to use the term as a trademark for his best prints, but it later suffered at the hands of other less skilled makers.

His first Christmas cards were produced in 1874 and were exported to England where Christmas greeting cards had been in use since about 1860. In America, there had been some use of these imported cards, many of them bearing the imprint of Raphael Tuck & Co., an outstanding English firm in the field of artistic color printing. The American public, however, had remained largely indifferent to them.

In 1876 Prang tried out an assortment of Christmas cards here. They sold so well that he soon established annual competitions for designs which well-known artists entered. One was the artist Captain Harry Beard who painted the originals of most of Prang's prize holiday cards as well as those of his competitors. Captain Beard was the brother of Daniel Carter Beard who originated the Boy Scout movement and also wrote the famous *American Boys' Handy Book.*

These late nineteenth-century Christmas cards were, like the valentines of the time, elaborate creations. Some of them even sported silk fringe (Illustration 132). This double-faced card is five and one-quarter by four and one-half inches and framed with a one-inch fringe. Done by a contemporary of Prang's, "Wirths Bros. & Owen," about 1885, it shows two Old-World scenes in soft pastel tones of brown, green, and grey-blue with traces of powdered mica for snow. One side shows a small country church and the other a little chapel, both with a large rayed five-point star in the upper corner. Lettering on one side includes "Christmas Greeting" and "Joy, Peace and Hope" and "God's blessing be with thee." Beneath each view appears "NO.256 Copyright" and the name of the lithographer.

In the late 1880's, cards with floral designs appeared, both single and double-faced, with and without fringe. These floral motifs caught the sentimental fancy of the time and because increasingly popular. From such modest beginnings, Louis Prang started something which he could neither have foreseen nor believed possible—the twentieth-century greeting-card industry.

# BIBLIOGRAPHY

## GENERAL

*American Antiques in Word and Picture*, Alice Winchester; published by the author, New York, 1943

*Collecting Antiques in America*, Thomas H. Ormsbee; The McBride Company, Inc., New York, 1940

*Decorative Art of Victoria's Era*, Frances Lichten; Charles Scribner's Sons, New York, 1950

*Handbook of Popular Antiques*, Katherine Morrison McClinton; Random House, New York, 1946

*Homes of Our Ancestors*, T. R. H. Halsey and Elizabeth Tower; Doubleday, Page and Company, Garden City, N. Y., 1925

*The Primer of Antiques*, Carl W. Drepperd; Doubleday, Doran & Company, Garden City, N. Y., 1944

## FURNITURE

*American Antique Furniture*, Edgar A. Miller, Jr.; The Lord Baltimore Press, Baltimore, Md., 1937

*The Book of American Clocks*, Brooks Palmer; The Macmillan Company, New York, 1950

*Colonial Furniture in America*, Luke Vincent Lockwood; third edition; Charles Scribner's Sons, New York, 1926

*Colonial Furniture of New England*, Irving W. Lyon; Houghton Mifflin Co., Boston, 1924

*Field Guide to American Victorian Furniture*, Thomas H. Ormsbee; Little, Brown and Company, Boston, 1952

*Field Guide to Early American Furniture*, Thomas H. Ormsbee; Little, Brown and Company, Boston, 1951

*Furniture Treasury*, Wallace Nutting; The Macmillan Company, New York, 1948. A reissue in two volumes of earlier three volumes, 1928-1933

*Practical Book of Period Furniture*, Harold D. Eberlein and Abbott McClure; J. B. Lippincott Company, Philadelphia, 1914

*The Story of American Furniture*, Thomas H. Ormsbee; The Macmillan Company, New York, 1934

## CHINA

*American Historical Views on Staffordshire China*, Ellouise B. Larsen; Doubleday, Doran & Company, New York, 1939

*Ceramics for the Collector*, George Savage; Rockliff, London, 1949

*Collecting Old English Lustre*, Jeannette R. Hodgen; The Southworth-Anthoensen Press, Portland, Me., 1937

*Dresden China*, W. B. Honey; A. & C. Black Ltd., London, 1934

*English Pottery and Porcelain*, W. B. Honey; A. & C. Black Ltd., London, 1933

*Marks and Monograms on European and Oriental Pottery and Porcelain*, William Chaffers, edited by Frederick Litchfield; fourteenth edition; The Borden Publishing Company, Los Angeles, Calif., 1946

*Old Pottery and Porcelain*, Fred W. Burgess; G. P. Putnam's Sons, New York, 1916

*Oriental Lowestoft*, J. A. Lloyd Hyde; Charles Scribner's Sons, New York, 1939

*The Practical Book of Chinaware*, Harold D. Eberlein and Roger W. Ramsdell; J. B. Lippincott Company, Philadelphia, 1925

*Staffordshire Pottery*, Josiah Wedgwood and Thomas H. Ormsbee; The McBride Company, Inc., New York, 1947

*Wedgwood*, John M. Graham II and Hensleigh C. Wedgwood; Tudor Publishing Company, New York, 1948

### GLASS

*American Glass*, George S. and Helen McKearin; Crown Publishers, New York, 1941

*Cambridge Glass*, Lura Woodside Watkins; Little, Brown and Company, Boston, 1930

*Early American Pressed Glass*, Ruth Webb Lee; published by the author, Framingham, Mass., 1931

*English and Irish Glass*, W. A. Thorpe; The Medici Society, Boston, 1927

*Old Glass Paperweights*, Evangeline H. Bergstrom; The Lakeside Press, Chicago, Ill., 1940

*Opaque Glass*, S. T. Millar, M.D.; Central Press, Topeka, Kan., 1941

*Sandwich Glass*, Ruth Webb Lee; published by the author, Framingham Centre, Mass., 1939

*Victorian Glass*, Ruth Webb Lee; published by the author, Northboro, Mass., 1941

### SILVER

*American Plated Silver*, Larry Freeman and Jane Beaumont; Century House, Watkins Glen, N. Y., 1947

*American Silversmiths and Their Marks*, Stephen G. C. Ensko; Robert Ensko Inc., New York, 1937

*The Book of Old Silver*, Seymour B. Wyler; Crown Publishers, New York, 1937

*Chaffer's Handbook to Hall Marks on Gold & Silver Plate*, Cyril G. E. Bunt, editor; seventh edition; William Reeves Bookseller Limited, London, 1945

*Early American Silver*, C. Louise Avery; D. Appleton-Century Company, New York, 1930.

*History of Old Sheffield Plate*, Frederick Bradbury; The Macmillan Company, New York, 1912

*Historic Silver of the Colonies and Its Makers*, Francis H. Bigelow; The Macmillan Company, New York, 1917

### PRINTS

*American Engravers on Copper and Steel*, David McN. Stauffer; The Grolier Club, New York, 1907

*America on Stone*, Harry T. Peters; Doubleday, Page and Company, Garden City, N. Y., 1931

*Currier & Ives, Printmakers to the American People*, Harry T. Peters; Doubleday, Doran & Company, Garden City, N. Y., 1942

*Early American Prints*, Carl W. Drepperd; D. Appleton-Century Company, New York, 1930

### PAINTING

*America's Old Masters*, James T. Flexner; The Viking Press, New York, 1939

*American Primitive Painting*, Jean Lipman; Oxford University Press, New York, 1942

*Early American Portrait Painters*, Cuthbert Lee; Yale University Press, New Haven, Conn., 1929

*The History of American Painting*, Samuel Isham; The Macmillan Company, New York, 1936

*Life in America*, The Metropolitan Museum of Art, New York, 1939

*Limners and Likenesses*, Alan Burroughs; Harvard University Press, Cambridge, Mass., 1936

*The Pocket History of American Painting*, James T. Flexner; Pocket Books, Inc., New York, 1950

### PEWTER

*American Pewter*, J. B. Kerfoot; Houghton Mifflin Co., Boston and New York, 1924

*Pewter in America*, Ledlie I. Laughlin; Houghton Mifflin Co., Boston and New York, 1940

### QUILTS AND COVERLETS

*Historic Quilts*, Florence Peto; American Historical Company, New York, 1939

*Old Patchwork Quilts and the Women Who Made Them*, Ruth E. Finley; J. P. Lippincott Company, Philadelphia, 1929.

*The Romance of the Patchwork Quilt in America*, Carrie A. Hall and Rose G. Kretsinger; Caxton Printers Ltd., Caldwell, Idaho, 1935

# INDEX